Writing Out Loud

The Twelve Commandments of Good Dictation

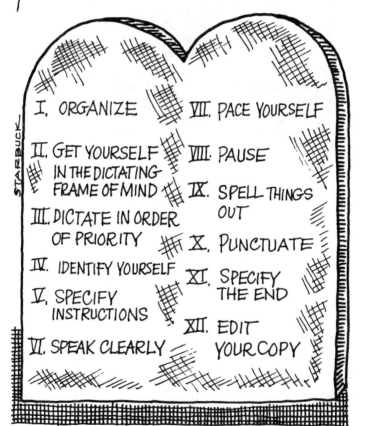

STARBUCK

I. ORGANIZE

II. GET YOURSELF IN THE DICTATING FRAME OF MIND

III. DICTATE IN ORDER OF PRIORITY

IV. IDENTIFY YOURSELF

V. SPECIFY INSTRUCTIONS

VI. SPEAK CLEARLY

VII. PACE YOURSELF

VIII. PAUSE

IX. SPELL THINGS OUT

X. PUNCTUATE

XI. SPECIFY THE END

XII. EDIT YOUR COPY

Writing Out Loud

The Time-Saving Art of Dictation

Jefferson D. Bates

ACROPOLIS BOOKS LTD.

ACROPOLIS BOOKS LTD.
11741 Bowman Green Dr.
Reston, VA 22090

Attention: Schools and Corporations
ACROPOLIS books are available at quantity discounts with bulk purchase for educational, business, or sales promotional use. For information, please write to SPECIAL SALES DEPARTMENT, ACROPOLIS BOOKS LTD., 11741 BOWMAN GREEN DRIVE, RESTON, VA 22090.

Are there Acropolis Books you want but cannot find in your local stores?
You can get any Acropolis book title in print. Simply send title and retail price. Be sure to add postage and handling: $2.25 for orders up to $15.00; $3.00 for orders from $15.01 to $30.00; $3.75 for orders from $30.01 to $100.00; $4.50 for orders over $100.00. Virginia residents add applicable sales tax. Enclose check or money order only, no cash please, to:

ACROPOLIS BOOKS LTD.
13950 Park Center Rd.
Herndon, VA 22071

Library of Congress
Cataloging-in-Publication Data

Bates, Jefferson D., 1920-
    Writing out loud.

    Previously published as: Dictating effectively.
    Includes bibliographical references and index.
    1. Dictation (Office practice). I. Title. HF 5547.5.B35 1990 651.7′4
90-14411 ISBN 0-87491-966-5

Dedication

To Poggy, my favorite dictator,
and to Bill and Stacy, who help her.

Table of Contents

Dost thou love life,
then do not squander time,
For time's the stuff life's made of.
— Benjamin Franklin

Foreword by J. Willard Marriott, Jr.

My experience with dictation is almost entirely from the management viewpoint, but I am increasingly aware of how beneficial it can be to persons in other occupations. I believe that busy persons get much more done than those who don't have much to do—because the busier they get, the more they learn to organize themselves to use time effectively.

An excellent book called *The Time Trap*, by R. Alec Mackenzie, taught me some useful techniques for organizing myself—but didn't say much about the benefits of dictation as a time-saving tool. That's why *Writing Out Loud* (formerly titled *Dictating Effectively*) now takes its place beside *The Time Trap* as a new and valuable aid in helping me make the most of my working time.

I've always found that one of the greatest time wasters for most people is PROCRASTINATION. Dictation can be a major tool in conquering that problem. The mark of the true professional is the ability to respond effectively to big challenges as well as to small ones. Almost anyone can deal adequately with small problems and short jobs. But many persons push back difficult big jobs because they appear so formidable in terms of time required. "That job will take too long—I'll tackle it the first thing tomorrow." And tomorrow never comes.

I've discovered that with dictation, anyone can conquer procrastination. Using the techniques described in *Writing Out Loud,* it's easy to break the biggest task into small, easy-to-handle bits and pieces. I have a project on my desk right now. For several days, I've been collecting information and dictating bits and pieces about it; soon I'll be ready to fit all the pieces together. With all the facts transcribed before me, I'll be in a position to finish the whole project quickly—probably tomorrow. And that's a tomorrow that *will* come.

I've found it is important to pick a time of day when you're really at your best, then tackle the toughest jobs first. I've also discovered, however, that ideas often come—unexpected and uninvited, but welcome—at the strangest times. I write them down on 3x5 cards—always keep a bundle of them in my pocket. Then I use the cards to dictate later. My brother Richard, however, often puts many of his thoughts straight onto the tape. He says that his tiny, pocket-size tape recorder has become his constant companion. He carries it with him almost everywhere—even on airplane flights. He also carries several extra tapes. Then, even if he is in the middle of other dictation, if a good idea strikes him, he removes the cassette, snaps in a fresh one, and captures the idea before it gets away. He tells me he even dictates ideas in his car while waiting for a light to change.

My dictation is more likely to take place in the office. I find I work best when I can organize for it in advance. It's worth the effort to take a few minutes to sort out thoughts before starting to dictate.

I learned to dictate by trial and error, the same way almost everyone else I know had to learn, because *Writing Out Loud* had not yet been written. I agree with its concepts: I have found from experience, for example, that I do a much better job when I have jotted down a list of ideas before I start to dictate. If I take time to write down priority items and make notes about them, the dictation itself comes much more easily—and much more logically. When my secretary gives the transcribed draft back to me (if it's more than a one-paragraph letter I always ask for a draft first), everything can be quickly edited into shape. It's worth every second of the time it takes—not all that much—and I can then be sure I've said exactly what I intended to say. I can finish the job quickly and get on with something else.

But dictation is just *one* tool — and it's not the *only* tool. In fact, I avoid the need for a lot of dictation because my secretary has learned to compose routine letters. She can turn out acknowledgments, thank-you notes, and much other routine correspondence better than I could do it myself, thus freeing me to handle the projects that require my personal attention.

I deliberately strive not to overdo the dictation, because I find it is almost too easy. I constantly guard against the danger of overloading my secretary with unnecessary detail, thus losing much of the efficiency that dictation offers.

I don't keep any job on my desk except the one I'm actually working on. What is there I intend to get done TODAY. I don't like to leave my office until the desk is clean, and dictation is one of the best ways I know to do it.

Finally, although I've been dictating for years, *Writing Out Loud* has shown me that I have not yet learned to use the tool to its fullest advantage. For example, I've never dictated a speech. Following the advice set forth in Chapter Thirteen, you can be sure that I'll dictate my next one.

No, dictation is not a panacea. It is not *the* answer to effective time management. But it is *an* answer, and an extremely good one. I heartily recommend *Writing Out Loud* to anyone who wants to find more useful hours in every working day.

—J. Willard Marriott, Jr.
July 24, 1980

Speak the speech I pray you,
trippingly on the tongue.
— Hamlet

Author's Non-Preface

"Nobody reads prefaces nowadays," Al Lefcowitz said.

"Wrong!" I said. "I always do."

"You read the labels on tomato cans," Al said.

Al was right. As usual. That's why I'm calling this a "Non-Preface." Please think of it only as a convenient place for me to ask a question before you turn to Chapter One. (The question isn't hard, and besides, I'll help you with the answer. Is that fair or what?)

QUESTION: Is it easier for most people to talk than it is to write?
(Substitute the word "you" for "most people," if the substitution makes the question easier to answer.)
ANSWER: Most people find it far easier to talk — they learn to talk years before they learn to write.

Psychologists tell us that the brain is "pre-programmed" for mastering speech skills. That's why some precocious babies learn to talk before their first birthday, and most of the rest begin communicating fluently before reaching the age of two.

But writing is an acquired skill: clumsy young fingers usually aren't ready to begin their on-going struggles with penmanship (or pencilmanship or crayonmanship) until the student to whom they are attached enters the first grade. Sometimes it takes a good deal longer than that. (Apologies for using the sexist word "penmanship." I couldn't think of a suitable word to replace it.)

Only after years of hard work and continuing effort do students learn to let their thoughts flow—via the writing instrument—onto the paper. Neither "pen/pencil/crayon/manship" nor writing comes naturally, the way speech does. So it shouldn't be too surprising that most people don't learn to write (in either sense of the word) particularly well, and they seldom find it easy to do.

Writing has been my life's work. I've spent most of the last 40 years trying to teach myself, and others, to write better. My book *Writing With Precision*, which was intended to sum up all my experience, has been called a classic, or so I've been told. (Of course, my hero, Mark Twain, once said that a classic is a book nobody reads—sort of like a preface—so I'll try not to get swellheaded.

But late in life, I discovered that *Writing With Precision* hasn't "said it all"—at least not all I want to say. *Writing Out Loud* is its logical sequel. *WOL* is really as much about writing as it is about dictation, because I have come to realize that the two skills go together. Now all I have to do is persuade the rest of the world.

Sometimes the simplest truths are hardest for us to see. I always thought learning to dictate was hard, and for me it was, because I had hang-ups. But if you go about it right, learning to dictate is easy, because dictation is based on inherent *speech* skills.

This book will help you go about it right. Dictation can give your *writing* much of the ease and fluency of speech. And wild as this statement may seem to you, it can change your life. It has certainly changed mine!

All the world's a stage ...
— Shakespeare

Cast of Characters

"How about acknowledgments?" I said. "At least I have to put in acknowledgments — give credit where credit is due."

"Nobody reads them either."

I guess Al couldn't stand my pained expression. "Maybe you could compromise by putting in a 'Cast of Characters.'" (Al is a playwright.) "You're always putting the names of people in your books, and at least that way everybody will know who everybody else is."

He's right about that too. I hate books that don't have people in them, and I always enjoy reading my own books because they are peopled with such nice people.

So this is really the *Acknowledgments* section, but Al said nobody would read it if I called it that. Besides, it's fun to have a *Cast of Characters* for a book instead of for a play.

All of the characters listed here are real.[1] In addition to those named, there are many others who have aided me whose names I do not know. I wish I did — I'd like to acknowledge their helpfulness in answering my questions about dictation, making suggestions for additions and corrections, and generally giving me the benefit of their knowledge.

Robert "Bob" Allen (retired) — A friend and former neighbor, Bob retired some years ago from the Office of Academic Affairs, Hq., U.S. Veterans Administration. Bob not only criticized my manuscript, but played an important role in helping me get needed information about technical, medical, and legal dictation, putting me in touch with Mr. Jack Blasingame and Ms. Patricia Teernstra, also of the VA.

James R. "Jim" Aswell (deceased) — My longtime friend and mentor, a writer of fiction and nonfiction under more than 50 pen names, humorist (*Native American Humor*), Rosenwald fellow, and the best editor I've ever known.

"Poggy" Bates — My wife, whose real name is Margaret. Most Margarets are nicknamed Peggy, but not Poggy. She deserves special thanks because she taught herself to transcribe dictation especially for this project, and has served as guinea pig and critic for my dictation experiments and far-out theories. Thanks also to my daughter **Stacy** and my son **Bill**, who — although not mentioned specifically in the text — have done their best to get their father straightened out.

Art "Mr. Lucky" Fettig — Professional speaker and writer who has worked with my partner, Lou Hampton, at several national conferences and conventions. Art coined Lou's slogan, "The pro who makes pros better."

Alphons "Al" Hackl (retired) — My good friend who was my publisher for the first edition. I owe thanks to Al for his understanding and patience. Thanks also to many members of his staff at Acropolis, including **Robert Hickey, Allyson Everngam, Suzanne Dunn, Laurie Dustman Tag, Sandy Alpert,** and **Sandy Trupp.** (For the new edition, my thanks to Al's successors at Acropolis, **John Hackl** and **Kathleen Hughes**, publishers, and to editor **Lynne Shaner** for her skilled blue (actually, red!) pencil.

Louis J. "Lou" Hampton — My friend and once my partner, now head of his own firm. Lou is a professional speaker and speech coach, seminar leader, and an expert at dictation.

Laura Horowitz (deceased) — the founder and president of Editorial Experts, Inc. One of the most talented human beings and best editors I have ever known. Some of the members of her staff who also contributed are **Floyd Anderson, Delores Ault, Carol Hawley, Peggy Smith, and Rufus Smith.**

James J. "Jim" Jeffries — (formerly) Manager of Organization and Personnel Development, The Coca-Cola Company (Foods Division), now a freelance artist, sculptor, photographer, and writer. Jim and I collaborated some years ago on a book entitled *Executive's Guide to Conferences, Meetings, and Audiovisual Presentations.*

Virgil Carrington "Pat" Jones — (retired) My friend and colleague from NASA (National Aeronautics and Space Administration) days. Pat is a gifted editor, an expert dictator, and the most disciplined writer I've ever encountered. He is the author of many books, including *Ranger Mosby, Gray Ghosts and Rebel Raiders,* and *The Hatfields and the McCoys.*

Allan "Al" Lefcowitz — Good friend, topflight writer, editor, and critic. He is also a poet, a playwright, the founder and director of the Writer's Center, and a professor of English at the U.S. Naval Academy.

Ina Lerner — Ina is a management consultant who has worked with Hampton & Bates as director of planning and operations. A former teacher of business skills, she knows about dictation from both sides of the desk.

Robert "Bob" Orben — Bob is best known as the world's number one expert on comedy writing. Less known to the general public is the fact that he is an excellent writer, a marketing expert, and a former Presidential speechwriter. In 1979 he was winner of Acropolis' Annual Zero Base Gobbledygook Award.

Carl Sieg (retired) — management expert, seminar leader, and formerly a senior associate of Hampton & Bates. Carl has held top personnel jobs in both government and industry, and is one of the most efficient dictators I know.

Shirley Starbuck — A talented artist and a lovely lady. I'm proud to have her as the illustrator for this book.

Charles "Chuck" Waterman — My friend and former colleague, intrepid editor, demon researcher, and now my successor as president of Speak/Write Systems.

ADDITIONAL ACKNOWLEDGMENTS

Thanks also to **Bruce Boston, Phyllis Burbank, Patricia Harris, Jodie Hester, Jack and Nancy Kelso, Stuart Kravits, Werner Low, Joe Proctor, Susan Price,** and **Don Till.**

Living is entirely too time-consuming.
— Irene Peter, quoted in
Peter'sQuotations

1: How to Beat the Time Trap — Dictate!

Timeliness Is Next to Godliness

Do you often yearn for more hours in the day? Wonder how to finish that report before deadline without working all night? Dread facing that mountain of letters overflowing in your in-basket, and despair of ever cutting it down to a molehill?

Welcome to the Time Trap Club. Its millions of members are mostly people who can't or won't learn to dictate. I belonged for years. Now I've resigned; please join me as a Member Emeritus, mastering time instead of letting it master us.

You'll increase your work output in both quantity and quality. As a bonus, dictation skills will help you find time to tackle neglected projects long simmering on the back burner.

Beat the time trap — learn to dictate. You'll never regret it; once you master the art, you can double, triple, perhaps even quadruple your daily writing output. Even better, you'll perform *all* your work assignments more easily. Let me tell you what dictation skills can do for you.

Time Out for a Flashback

Most people don't dictate. Sorry about that, but it's a fact of life. I think it's a real pity. Worse than that, it's a waste. It seems so obvious (at least to me) that *everyone whose work involves writing should learn how to dictate.* But — repeating for emphasis — *most people don't dictate*, and those who do often don't take full advantage of dictation's many benefits and possibilities.

If you are a member of that group of "most people," this book can change your life. I know this sounds like hype, but please bear with me. I have seldom been more serious about anything in my life. A few paragraphs of personal history will tell you why.

I dictated the original version of this book, then entitled *Dictating Effectively*, more than ten years ago. Yes, I *dictated*, not *wrote*, every word in the first draft. (That's the answer to the first question most people ask.)

At that time, I had been a professional writer for more than 30 years — BUT I had never dictated before. Indeed, I had always been afraid to try. Then, within six weeks, I taught myself to dictate and put my newly acquired skills to the ultimate test.

I'm still proud of *Dictating Effectively,* which, according to letters from many readers, has played a seminal role in their lives. (Many followed my example and have dictated books of their own.) But after ten more years of dictating experience, I'm embarrassed at one major misjudgment I made. Out of inexperience (okay, sheer ignorance!), I aimed at an audience that was much too narrow — executives with heavy correspondence loads, doctors making hospital rounds, lawyers preparing legal briefs, and so on.

I have since learned that professional dictating skills can help ANYONE who writes — not just the business executives and professionals that I used to think of as the only persons who can use dictation as a time-saving tool. If anything, the skill is often even more useful for professional writers — novelists, playwrights, poets, advertising copy writers, speechwriters, and a host of others, whether they specialize in fiction or nonfiction.

I promise at least one of the following benefits to every reader who follows my advice:

- If you already dictate, this book will help you improve your skill (and your transcriber's disposition.)
- If you are a beginner or a student, this book will save you the wasted time and motion of having to learn by trial and error.
- If you suffer from "dictaphobia," the fear of dictating, this book will help you overcome that fear.

Case History of a Chronic Non-Dictator

During the Apollo program, when I headed the speechwriting and correspondence branches of the National Aeronautics and Space Administration (NASA), only a few colleagues shared my secret—I suffered from acute *dictaphobia*, an almost pathological fear of dictating. This malady, I have later found, is as common as the common cold. However, in interviewing scores of fellow victims of dictation hang-up, I have yet to find a case as chronic as mine, which lasted for more than 20 years.

Some people I interviewed had never had a problem and couldn't understand why anyone should. But continued questioning disclosed that at least two out of five executives share the fear of dictation; they may not admit that fear, but the tipoff is that they write everything in longhand—or, in my case—on a typewriter or word processor.

Thank You, Lady Luck!

Life patterns can be altered sharply by something as minor as an airline seat assignment. In January 1979, I took a flight to Houston to lead a writing seminar. On the plane, I was seated beside a personable chap who struck up an instant conversation. Even before takeoff, I learned that he makes his living as a professional writer. After the first martini, he started regaling me about the benefits of dictation. Having himself only recently learned the art, the evangelistic new convert rhapsodized about producing more and better copy than he used to, and spending less time doing it.

Saving time! Increasing production! Improving quality!

Those magic words jolted my nerve endings like a whack between the ears with a two-by-four. Till then, I hadn't given the art of dictation a thought. For years I had always typed my own manuscripts; because I'm a fast typist, I theorized that it made economic sense to compose directly on my word processor. Faced with constant short-fuze deadlines, I had always skipped the time-devouring steps of scribbling rough drafts and handing them to a secretary, as most of my colleagues did. I took pride in cranking my work out fast; it never occurred to me that any other method could be faster or better.

But my seatmate gently pointed out that when I was supposedly typing 70 or 80 words a minute—which I can do for a short spell when I'm going full blast—I undoubtedly wasn't spending much of the total time *typing*. "Don't try to kid me," he said. "I used to compose directly on a typewriter, too. Spent a lot of time looking at the blank page or staring at the ceiling, and wasting reams of paper typing 'Now is the time for all good men.' "

Then he pinned me down. "How many pages a day do you average, week in and week out?"

"Usually between five and ten," I said. "On good days, a lot more than that."

"Yeah, and on bad ones a lot less."

I had to admit he was right.

"Try dictating," he said. "Once you get the hang of it, you'll produce more copy than you ever thought possible. That's a promise!"

By the time we landed in Houston, I was as sold as he was—couldn't wait to get home and try dictating again: once more unto the breach!

Getting Out of the Time Trap

I once read an article about a management specialist who made this thought-provoking observation: most people don't think in terms of anything as small as minutes, so they waste an unconscionable number of minutes. On the other hand, they never think in terms of a whole life, either. Pursuing that parallel gets too depressing to contemplate. I'll leave it for my book on philosophy—when I get around to dictating it!

Most of us plan our work—and our living—in terms of hours or days. You know the story all too well: start over again every week, and spend another segment of our meager lifetime allotment of minutes, hours, and days on things not remotely related to our lifetime goals—assuming we have any.

Having already wasted enough time for any one person, I don't want you to follow my (former) bad example. Remedial action is definitely in order. If you and I are going to accomplish everything we aspire to, we must get on with the job.

Fortunately, I can now offer you the key, which came to me as a result of that fateful flight to Houston. Waiting in the airport's baggage area, I had ample time to ponder the fleeting minutes even more. As I watched everyone's luggage but mine tumble onto the carrousel, my subconscious mind started piecing the puzzle together: *Save the minutes! Get control of your time, what's left of it! Dictating can do it!*

Then it was still theory. Now it is proven fact. The art of dictating opened for me a whole new world: one with more useful hours in the day. What my enthusiastic seatmate told me is true: a skilled dictator turns out the equivalent of a full day's writing production (by the old standards) in as little as 30 minutes.

Using dictation, I can easily surpass my most productive former output. (In fact, I dictated the entire first draft of this book in about three weeks.) The material must still be transcribed, of course, but that task can be delegated. What a kick to devote full attention to *creation* with no worries about *mechanics.* Can't beat that!

After ten years of heavy dictating almost every day, I've captured enough fleeting minutes to pass on to you this heartfelt conviction:

> # Dictating Is a Terrific Way To Get MORE Done in LESS Time.

That thought may not be elegantly expressed, but please inscribe it on your memory in letters of gold.

The art of dictation enables us to use the day's most productive hours for creative endeavors. In my case, it allows ample time to read the paper, drink my coffee, shoot the breeze with colleagues, and still turn out a full stint of writing every day.

And that brings us to the closing thought for this chapter. During a conversation about beating the time trap, Chuck Waterman suggested the following quotation as a fitting wrap-up:

> ## The task that is the most URGENT is not always the most IMPORTANT.

Once you grasp the significance of this thought, watch your priorities start falling neatly into place.

If something is worth doing, it is worth
telling someone how to do it well.
— Franklin P. Jones, in
      The Wall Street Journal

2: Writing Out Loud

Dear Fellow Writers:

Have you ever written an article while you were on board an aircraft? Turned out the first draft of a short story while taking a walk on a beautiful sunny day? Or dashed off some ideas on a novel while lying in bed at night after you've come up with an exciting plot idea that just won't let you sleep?

I have — many times. But chances are, sad to say, you almost certainly have not. This isn't just a wild guess on my part. Since the first edition of this book came out ten years ago, I've interviewed more than 300 professional writers, including some highly successful ones, and asked them the same questions I just asked you. And I dictated this new chapter — on board an airplane en route to Seattle, as it happens — largely because of the answers they gave me.

To get straight to the point, I found out that many professional writers use tape recorders in their work, one way or another. But as a group, they're just like the "most people" I talked about in Chapter One. Almost none of them use DICTATION as a technique to capture their ideas and make it easier to get them down on paper. Odds are about 100-to-1 that you're in the same boat. It's time you did something about it. String along with me and read the rest of this chapter, and your writing life will never be the same again. Just follow the plan I outline. I guarantee that you can double — maybe even triple — your writing production.

The Greatest Little Time-Saver Ever

It's time for you to discover what many business executives already know. Dictation is one of the greatest time-savers ever invented for transferring ideas from your mind and making it easy to get them down on paper. You know as well as I do that the fastest of writers can't put down more than 20 words or so a minute onto paper with pen or pencil. And often your inspired production limps to a halt when you develop writer's cramp — one of the occupational hazards of our business.

To speed your production, many of you probably do the same thing that I did myself for the first 25 years of my career as a professional writer. That is, you learn to compose directly on a keyboard. If you are fast (and I am), you can type anywhere from 40 words a minute up to maybe even a 100 or more. That adds up to some very fast production, at least in theory. But don't fool yourself. You and I both know that we don't compose that fast, or anywhere near it.

Of course not. We often have to stop and ponder. There are frequent long pauses between flurries. What's worse we compose a beautiful paragraph in the mind, only to find that memory of the exact wording fails as the fingers struggle to keep up. It's always a losing battle.

That used to happen to me all the time. It happens to ALL writers.

Well, suppose that instead of pen or typewriter, you have a cassette recorder in your hand. That way, with no mechanical barriers to interfere, your voice readily keeps up with your fast-flowing thoughts. The words are captured on tape, from which they can be easily transcribed to paper.

Thinking Out Loud

Using dictation to get your first draft on paper — I call this thinking out loud — is so simple and easy and time-saving that I can't imagine why all writers don't use it. But, as I have discovered through lengthy research, in actuality, almost none of them do. Many of the business executives I know use dictation machines all the time — perhaps not always as effectively as they might, but they use them — and they save hours and increase productivity every day.

Writing the Hard Way

Some years ago I attended a writer's conference and workshop sponsored by the Washington Independent Writers, whose membership is made up of many of the most successful professional writers in the Washington, D.C., metropolitan area. It was an exciting experience to be able to talk informally and to exchange ideas with some of the writers whose names are household words in the business. For example, the first panel discussion I attended was led by four writers, including a best-selling novelist, a prize-winning biographer, and two well-known writers of nonfiction.

From their remarks I picked up many useful ideas. The novelist told us, for example, how he puts his background and research material for each chapter in a separate folder, and tackles each one as the mood strikes, not necessarily in order. I use a similar system myself, and it works fine.

But as I listened to his remarks about how long it takes him to get his first draft down on paper, and what his average daily production amounts to, I began to wonder. As well organized and successful as he obviously is, in my opinion he is definitely still doing things the hard way.

'Quill Pen' Productivity Standards

Next we heard from the prize-winning biographer. Again, I was deeply impressed by her methods, her scholarship, and the thoroughness of her approach. Her words are polished jewels, her published works are the epitome of professionalism. But again she told us, almost pridefully, how long she had to labor over each page as she was putting her first draft down on paper.

With the other speakers, the story was essentially the same. Over and over, I kept hearing that an output of 500 to 1000 words a day of decent copy is up to the highest standards of professional productivity.

That may have been true in the days of Mark Twain and Charles Dickens, but today we live in a different world. When was the last time you saw a quill pen? With today's many aids to efficiency and creativity, anyone who still writes with a pen or pencil, or who pecks away at a typewriter, is going through life driving an oxcart instead of flying a jet.

Let me finish my story. When the formal presentation was over and the floor was opened to the question-and-answer sessions, I asked the panelists: "Do any of you ever dictate your first drafts to save time?"

Not one of the panelists did.

While I had the floor, I addressed the same question to the audience of almost 150 writers assembled in the auditorium. One lonely hand went up, and that was it.

During the coffee break that followed, I hurried to seek out the owner of that solitary raised hand. I was extremely glad to get a chance to talk with this vital and interesting woman, whose name you would probably recognize. She was a successful freelance writer who had attained national recognition by writing books and articles on health subjects — and from her own experience, the pros and cons of radical mastectomy. This is a subject she wrote about with power and passion. It also happened to be, she told me, the reason she had learned to dictate in the first place. After her operation, she found typing painful. But driven by the desire to put her experiences on paper, and to help others, she taught herself to dictate. She grimaced as she told me, haltingly, how she had been extremely self-conscious when she started. She confided that at first she had locked herself in the bathroom and whispered into her cassette recorder so softly that no one would be able to listen to her.

Dictaphobia — The 'Freeze Syndrome'

I told her that we had something in common. Both of us had suffered from what is described by psychologists as "dictaphobia" — the fear of dictating. Such persons "freeze" when they pick up a microphone. I've talked with scores of these fellow sufferers. I know now that as many as four in ten of the persons reading this chapter share the same hang-up. In all my interviews, I've found this is the reason most writers give me when I ask them why they don't dictate their drafts.

Okay, if that's your problem, the next few pages set forth some easy, painless ways to get started. If you try these and *still* have problems, go on to my proven, never-fail system, spelled out step by step in Chapter Four.)

they may be less than perfect. After all, you tell yourself, they are just my first-draft efforts, and I can edit them later. That's true, and it is also a key concept of all good writing. Writing and editing use different parts of your brain, and it is a mistake to try to do both at the same time if you want to be either creative or productive.

But when you dictate, you become much more self-conscious and self-critical. You're afraid that you'll say things that don't come up to your own concept of quality. As a result, you find yourself criticizing every word before you have even said it. No wonder the machine terrifies you. But it's not really the machine at all — you just think it is. What is really hanging you up is the fear that you won't sound like a literary genius when the tape is played back. Don't worry about it. Even a literary genius (and for all I know, you may be one) doesn't turn out perfect copy on the first try. And that, after all, is what dictation is.

STEP ONE: Use Your Recorder for Interviews

For you professional writers, the easiest way to start is with an extremely simple practical use of your friendly little helper, the pocket dictation machine. No doubt you now regularly carry index cards or a pad and pencil (or pen) in your coat pocket or purse when you go out to interview someone. Next time, take along your dictation machine too. That way, you can capture the actual words of the interview on the tape, and note on the pad the index numbers[1] that will make particular items easy for you to find when you play back the tape.

The advantages of recorded interviews are many — but don't just take my word for this. According to an article I read in an old issue of *Writer's Digest* when I was leafing though my collection, a Cincinnati writer named Willard Bailey says he has "the fastest tape recorder in the West." (Like most of the writers I've interviewed personally with my tape recorder,

---

1   Most dictation machines have a resettable indexing indicator similar to the trip odometer on your car. Set the numbers to zero at the beginning of the tape, and it's easy to index points on the tape you want to be able to find quickly.

Bailey uses his — he always carries two — solely for interviewing. I'm glad he's spreading the gospel about taping interviews, but by limiting his recorder to this single-purpose use, he's still doing things the hard way.)

At any rate, Bailey's article showed that he has the techniques of taping interviews well under control. As he explained, by using the tape recorder he is totally free to converse with the interviewee. That way he has plenty of time to think about what questions to ask next. Also, says Bailey, "it offers blessed relief from writer's cramp."

My search through back issues hit more pay dirt. I found that famed novelist Arthur Hailey uses a different interviewing technique.[2] When he does the research for one of his painstakingly thorough books such as *Wheels* or *Airport,* he interviews scores of people to get background information. However, he explains, he makes it a point not to take along a tape recorder, or even a note pad, feeling that these tools might inhibit the interviewee. Instead, he relies solely on his memory, which obviously must be a helluva lot better than mine. Then, after the interview, he rushes back to his trusty tape recorder and dictates all his mental notes while the memory is still fresh. His secretary then transcribes the notes and he files them away with the other raw material for his work in progress. He says the system works fine. He also says (my emphasis added) *that he does not dictate his actual drafts.* Mr. Hailey, I admire your work, but I think you've missed a bet.

These are professional, working writers who know whereof they speak. Even though I may disagree with minor points of their techniques, I have profited from their words, and I hope you will also. Now for step two:

STEP TWO: Keep an Audio Notebook

My old friend Virgil Carrington (Pat) Jones, author of *Ranger Mosby, Gray Ghosts and Rebel Raiders,* and many other books, is the first professional writer I know to have used a cassette recorder for notetaking. Back in the 60s when we were working side by side at NASA, Pat bought a

---

2 I have long since discovered that I can't do it his way myself, but it obviously works fine for him.

cassette recorder just a few months after those marvelous machines first came on the market. Far ahead of the crowd, as he usually is, he routinely carried the device with him. For example, when he went to the Library of Congress to research his "work in progress" at that time — *Roosevelt's Rough Riders*, published by Doubleday — Pat skipped the step of taking handwritten notes. Instead, he would read off all his reference materials and sources quickly onto the tape. By transcribing the information later at home, he speeded up his research process enormously.

I have profited by Pat's example in that and many other ways. I know now that any writer who has the foresight to keep a recorder handy can capture any idea that comes to mind, day or night. Take it with you in your car, or even on an airplane flight.

Have it in reach on your bedside table at night, so you can catch the inspiration that awakens you from your dreams — or more accurately, that comes to you in your dreams. You know, those wonderful ideas that you can never quite recall when you try to remember them in the morning. I'm not suggesting that you let midnight dictation break up your marriage. My wife Poggy "explained" to me that it might be a good idea for me to go in the bathroom and shut the door if I couldn't modulate my glorious baritone sufficiently to stop disturbing her dreams. (Actually, not long after that I discovered that you can whisper softly into a closely held mike and record every word clearly, without bothering a soul.)

My greatest all-time "case history" took place in January 1981, just before *Dictating Effectively* came out. I was still a rank beginner at dictation at the time. I was flying from Washington National Airport to Seattle to lead a writing seminar there. As an experiment, I decided to put dictation to the test by seeing how much I could dictate during a transcontinental flight (including a one-hour layover in Kansas City.)

The results positively amazed me; I turned out five separate pieces, each later to be a magazine article or a book chapter. For example, the first draft of this chapter,[3] plus the chapter entitled "Dreaming Out Loud," were both

---

3 First published in pamphlet form by Speak/Write Systems, Inc., ©1982. That version is no longer in print.

finished during the first leg of the flight. Another piece, an article that was published by Delta Airlines in its "Flying Colonels" newsletter, described some of my experiences and suggestions for business executives to dictate in flight. And during the final two hours on the plane, I dictated two chapters of another work-in-progress, called "The Compleat Speechwriter — Backstage With a Washington Ghost." (I still haven't found a publisher for this book, but what do they know?)

The following night, after a full day of seminar work, I relaxed by dining in the famed "Space Needle" restaurant (built for the Seattle World's Fair) some 600 feet above the city. The view was breathtaking; night had fallen, and at first I didn't realize that the restaurant was turning slowly, like a giant phonograph turntable suspended in midair. One minute I was looking out across Puget Sound at the mighty Olympic mountains; a few ships were moving across the horizon, their lights reflected in the water. Then the view gradually began to change as the lights and magnificent skyline of the city itself slowly swung into view.

If you attribute the specific details contained in this description to my marvelously retentive memory, let me disillusion you. As I began writing this, I tried first to evoke in my mind the dramatic details of the view as I had seen it. But as much as I had been impressed at the time, I found that the picture was no longer sharp in my mind.

But as a part of my experiment, I had described the entire scene, and my impressions of it, on my trusty dictation machine. When I arrived home again and played back the tape that held my "eye-witness description," the difference between the taped on-the-spot description and my fading memories was profound.

I found the cassette contained all kinds of details that never would have occurred to me if I hadn't captured them in "audio snapshots," recording not only small things such as colors, sounds, and smells, but also some of the emotional or sense-oriented responses that came to me. How did a particular thing strike me? Did it evoke any kind of sensation or emotion?

Why don't you check things out for yourself?

We are such stuff
As dreams are made on . . .
— Shakespeare

3: Dreaming Out Loud

The Act of Creation

In 1973, after more than 25 years as a professional writer in the U.S. Civil Service, I retired from NASA. The glory years of the Apollo moon landings and Skylab had ended; in the hiatus that followed, my writing tasks no longer seemed urgent or exciting. Life was growing dull and commonplace. I decided the time had come to try my wings as a freelancer.

My assignments during the NASA years had been to write speeches and articles for high NASA officials, astronauts, and members of the House and Senate Space Committees. I often had to interview scientists or study highly technical, frequently obscure technical papers and reports on space-related or scientific subjects. My goal was to translate these convoluted monstrosities into speeches and articles that the lay public could read (or hear) and understand — as crisply, clearly, accurately, and entertainingly as I possibly could.

When I left NASA and became a freelancer, I had to make a living by continuing with many writing assignments of the same genre. The difference was that I was at last free to broaden my scope. I began to tackle

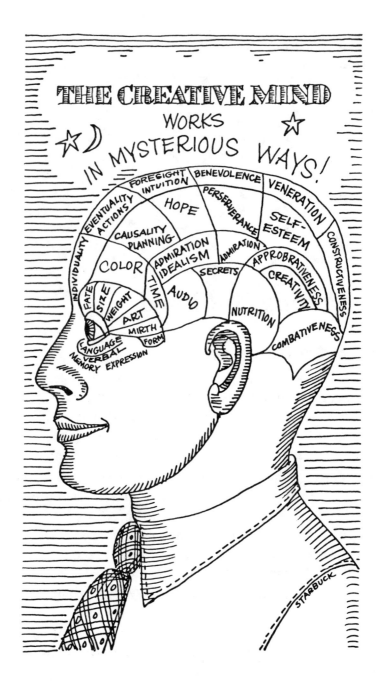

new, speculative projects that included short stories, a couple of how-to books, a serious novel, a thriller, and some light verse.

All of a sudden I found myself thinking more about what some writers nowadays call "controlled creativity." Where do ideas come from? How do works of the imagination originate? Is there any kind of workable system? Do creative geniuses think in a different way from the rest of us? Do the thought processes of mathematicians and, say, novelists, have anything in common? How do they go about evoking "the muse"?

I didn't know very many "creative" writers at the time.[4] But a few of the ones I *did* know told me that they had experienced an occasional "moment of truth." I knew what they were talking about. All too rarely, I had myself had brief flashes when what I was writing almost wrote itself, with little conscious thought or effort on my part.

I wanted to find out the secret. Could anyone learn how to become inspired "on call"?

That was when my old mentor, Jim Aswell, a gifted writer of both fiction and nonfiction, introduced me to a seminal book called *The Act of Creation*, by Arthur Koestler.[5] (If you haven't read it, please rush out and get a copy right away! I consider it a work of genius.)

Altered States of Consciousness

Koestler's book shook me to the core. It described, in fascinating detail, his research in seeking a common thread among great creative minds in the very act of creating. I suspect that Koestler had some flashes of his own. Digging for answers on the workings of this mysterious process, he pored over hundreds of diaries, journals, and other works that might illumine the process. His range was broad indeed; his subjects included artists, com-

---

4 Starting in 1978, I was fortunate enough to get to know, and learn from, many topflight poets, playwrights, and novelists at The Writer's Center; I even took courses from several of them, and proudly served on the WC Board of Directors until late in 1989.

5 My editor at Acropolis tells me this is now out of print. Try your public library or a secondhand bookstore.

posers, inventors, mathematicians, musicians, novelists, painters, poets, and various kinds of child prodigies.

All that digging paid off—Koestler's own brilliant creativity enabled him eventually to isolate patterns common to all these disparate geniuses. One way or another, usually accidentally or unknowingly, they had entered an altered state of consciousness—a trance-like, dream-like state.

Serendipity (or what C. E. Jung called "Synchronicity") then led me to some newly reported studies on altered states of consciousness. I stumbled onto some writings by a group of west coast psychological researchers. Most of their names have long since escaped me, but I remember that their leader was an innovative thinker named Charles Tart.

Reading these materials *really* shook me up. If I had interpreted their conclusions correctly, Dr. Tart and his colleagues were picking up where Koestler left off. They seemed to be offering a key to the kind of creativity that so many serious writers are constantly seeking, knowingly or unknowingly.

Once any writer experiences the phenomenon personally, life is never the same again. The foremost, all-important goal is to find a way to achieve the same effect again. All too often, the seekers find that "you can't get there from here." The harder one tries, the more difficult it often seems to reach this enraptured state. Total frustration sets in.

Creativity and the Alpha Level

Dr. Tart told about some experiments he had performed with machines that can read "brain waves," and detect the changes in frequencies that the brain emits when shifting from the so-called "beta level" (the "normal" alert waking state) to the "alpha level," where (so we are told) a wonderful creative power resides.

I thought to myself, what a marvelous world this would be if writers could get in touch with this creative level every time—or any time—that they wanted to. The frustrating inability to tap the vein of creativity has over the years plagued many of the greatest writers in our demanding trade. Some psychologists have speculated that this dreaded "block" probably drove Hemingway to suicide.

About that same time, I read an ad in, if I recall correctly, the *Saturday Review*. A mail-order outfit called J&J Enterprises in Washington state was offering a "poor person's EEG machine," and the price was under a hundred dollars. The ad was brief, but it stated that the device could detect brain waves and make them audible through earphones. This would permit the user to hear the differences in pitch or frequency that indicate an altered state of consciousness.

You are free to accept or reject as much or as little of what I say in the rest of this chapter as you please. You can skip it entirely and still learn to become an excellent dictator. I'm aware that some readers may find some of these ideas absurd. All I ask is that readers keep an open mind. I have described everything that happened as clearly and honestly as I can. As the cliché goes, "it works for me."

First Kid on the Block

During much of my government service, I worked with top scientists and engineers, authorities in many fields at the "cutting edge" of technology. My writing frequently involved translating difficult technical information into plain English for lay readers. I read dozens of scientific and technological publications every month. It was only natural that I became vitally interested in learning about new things; in my neighborhood, I was usually the "first kid on the block" to try new technology[6] — all the way from word processors and computers to "high fidelity" (long before "stereo").

So when I read about the EEG machine, I sent off for one right away. Sure enough, the machine appeared to do exactly what its makers had claimed it would. I kept on practicing with the biofeedback signals until I felt sure I was able to enter the alpha level at will. The changes in audio frequencies that I could hear in the earphones were clearly perceptible.

---

6 For example, I believe I was the first nonprofessional recordist on the East Coast to make live tape recordings in stereo. I recorded the Georgetown University Glee Club and the Air Force's "Airmen of Note" during the early 50s. I knew many of the musicians as friends, and — for a price — some of my engineer colleagues custom-built a two-channel recorder for me, many months — perhaps years — before similar machines became commercially available.

I found these experiments very exciting. Still I was not convinced that mastering this new ability had necessarily made me more creative. I'd go into the alpha level and try to write something, but my unconscious mind seemed just as uninspired as my conscious one. Where were all the works of genius that I had hoped were lurking down there someplace?

Still waiting impatiently for something to happen, I read an ad in *The Washington Post* about a seminar program called "Silva Mind Control." The ad said that the Silva courses were designed not only to teach students to enter the alpha level at will, but to put the ability to practical use.

I went to a free lecture. I wasn't too sure what to believe. The Silva instructors didn't use biofeedback—just a combination of breathing exercises, affirmations, and key words to recite to oneself. I was a bit dubious when I went home and tried it, but my EEG machine reassured me. It confirmed that the Silva technique seemed to work.

So I signed up for the course. I found that the Silva method, in its simplest terms, combines aspects of Asian philosophies—such as Yoga and Transcendental Meditation—with a sprinkling of autosuggestion and mental conditioning. (José Silva, upon whose research the seminars are founded, emphatically denies that his system involves any hypnosis or self-hypnosis. He emphasizes that *you* remain in control at all times. I think he's probably right about this, because I've always felt confident that I remain fully aware of whatever is going on.)

Having acquired some new pieces of the puzzle, I began setting aside a time each day to practice the Silva procedure. When I became fully relaxed, I'd write my thoughts down in a journal. Those thoughts, said the instructor, were emerging directly from the deeper levels—an altered state of consciousness.

The Silva instructor said the best routine is to close your eyes and then focus upward, inside your closed eyelids, to an angle about 45 degrees above the horizontal. Next, count backward from 10 to 1 (when you get the hang of it, you can just use 3 to 1), taking a deep breath or two between each count, and telling yourself to relax and go "deeper and deeper."

I discovered I could get better results if I kept my eyes shut. Unfortunately, the trouble was that—without being able to see to guide my pen—my handwriting was often so poor that I couldn't read it later.

(Another interesting phenomenon connected with all this was that—as I entered deeper and deeper levels of relaxation—my handwriting became progressively smaller until it became almost microscopic. A few days after the fact, I would find this handwriting almost impossible to read.)

Enter Dictation

I began to ask myself, "What would happen if I could somehow eliminate the artificial barriers between myself and the alpha level." But it was not until some seven years later that the question was finally resolved: after I taught myself to dictate, the final pieces of the puzzle fell into place.

After going through the routine described earlier, I would start dictating whatever came to my mind. I call this process "dreaming out loud," a variation of what Peter Elbow calls "free writing" in his useful book, *Writing Without Teachers*. (I strongly recommend that you read it.)

When you use a dictation machine, you automatically eliminate all mechanical barriers, including an important one I've only hinted at previously: it's impossible to write with a pen or pencil (or even a word processor) with anything remotely approaching the speed at which your mind is working. Inevitably you'll lose some thoughts, and some of your well-turned phrases (assuming you had any) are likely to get away from you entirely.

The dictation is easy to sustain, because you can keep your eyes closed. As pointed out earlier, if you open your eyes, you take the risk of losing some degree of concentration.

Summing Up—Creative Dictation (How to tap the alpha level)

1. Get in a comfortable position and relax. Many persons find it helpful to imagine themselves in a favorite place—perhaps a quiet spot under a tree or by a stream.

2. Close your eyes and tell yourself to relax. Then deepen your relaxation; some people tell themselves to relax their toes, their feet, their ankles, their calves, etc., working up to the top of the head.

3. Do a slow mental "countdown" from 10 to 1.

4. Breathe deeply between counts, and tell yourself to go "deeper and deeper."

5. Keep your eyes closed and roll them up 45 degrees (inside your eyelids) to help achieve alpha level.

6. With eyes still closed, start talking. Hold your dictation machine about six inches from your lips, but pay no attention to its presence. Talk conversationally.

7. Let your thoughts flow freely. Do not think about style or content.

Drawing on my fine command of the language,
I said nothing.
— Robert Benchley

4: Overcoming Dictaphobia

What's New?

This chapter was dictated on a battery-powered tape cassette recorder as I sat in my parked automobile.

Unusual? Not really. Books are often dictated this way. The one big difference is that for me it was like achieving the impossible dream.

This chapter explains how to master dictaphobia. In the three preceding chapters, I suggested some easy ways to get started. But if you are a really stubborn case, as I was, the exercises I'm about to set forth here are guaranteed to get you over the hurdles. By explaining the methods I used to overcome my own severe problems, I know positively that I can help any fellow dictaphobes do the same.

Do *you* shy away from dictation because you find it difficult? Does the mere thought send you into a panic? Or, on the other hand, do you consider yourself an exceptionally fluent dictator? Ponder the fact that "fluent" does not necessarily mean "good." The question is, when you dictate, is the product clear? Effective? To the point?

Be objective. If you can truthfully answer yes to all those questions, you may not need to bother with this chapter. If you're *really* that good, you may not even need this book. But if even a few negative responses showed up, this can help you.

Hang-ups — The 'Freeze' Syndrome

My interviews with dictators, would-be dictators, and dictaphobes have been enlightening. Now I know how common it is for usually articulate people to find themselves at a total loss for words — until they stop trying to dictate!

In the previous chapters, I referred to the "freeze" syndrome. This is apparently related to "mike fright," but not quite the same. The problem may not always be obvious to others, but it can cause as much misery as a sore tooth.

Analysis of the experiences of dozens of dictaphobes eventually disclosed the root of the problem: the moment we start trying to dictate we become overly self-conscious and self-critical — afraid that what we might say won't be perfect. Unconsciously, we try to edit each sentence before dictating it to the secretary or onto the tape.

No wonder the words stick in our throats. That mental censorship is sheer murder. As a writer, either in longhand or on the typewriter, I have long known that the secret of success is to get the first draft on paper *fast*. Keep the ideas flowing. Once those words are captured, you can edit them to your mind's content.

You Can Conquer Your Fright

With my newfound insights, I was at last able to give myself some good advice, which I now pass on to you:

RELAX. Turn off that nitpicking internal monitor and fire away. Remember, you can always straighten things out later. The printed version of my dictation that you are reading now is a whole lot different from the first raw copy. (It's a great comfort to know you can edit and re-edit your draft before you finally turn it loose.)

Read this one more time; take a few seconds to digest the thought. You won't believe it until you've checked things out for yourself, but I promise you faithfully that understanding and applying this advice is the first step towards conquering dictaphobia.

In a moment, I'll give you five KEYWORDS designed to pilot you safely past your fear of dictation. But first, let's psych up — it takes strong motivation to undergo the initial trauma — and frankly, that's what it is — of bracing for the drill.

You may think the old "positive thinking" slogans are malarkey. I won't argue with you, but I know it's much better to believe you CAN do something than to believe just as positively that you CAN'T. To learn to dictate, you must believe you *can* do it, and you must *want* to do it. So let me offer you a couple more reasons why you can't afford not to learn.

The first reason I have already told you — several times: *you can greatly multiply your daily writing output.* That alone should convince you.

But in some ways, this second reason is the real clincher: **you can make practical use of time that now isn't worth a thing to you or to anyone else — time that would otherwise be a total waste.**

(**NOTE:** *What follows — from here to the* **Summing Up** *section — is taken directly, and edited only lightly, from a transcription of my original dictation, done back in the fall of 1979. I used index cards to keep me on track with the keywords.)*

> As I sit here in my beat-up old VW, I am dictating this chapter. My carpool rider will be coming out soon, but he isn't in sight yet. In the days before dictation (from now on, I'll say "B.D." for short) I might have been daydreaming, listening to the radio, or just staring out the window. Instead, today I am dictating these words into my handy-dandy portable cassette recorder. The process is simple, painless, and (would you believe) fun. If there is an easier way to write a book I'd like to hear about it.
>
> Convinced? I hope so. Because now, if you really WANT to learn to dictate, you are ready for the five KEYWORDS that will put you on the road to dictation success. Here goes:

KEYWORD ONE – PRACTICE

The first important truth about beating dictaphobia is this: tell yourself that what you're doing is "just for practice" and doesn't really mean a thing. "Fake out" the analytical part of your mind that is holding you back.

If you have a hard time dictating your thoughts, try this: *read aloud into the microphone, using material someone else has written.* Start by reading a page or two, or whatever it takes; then go on talking about the same subject in your own words. Be sure to pick a familiar subject.

That approach helped me overcome my initial reluctance. I'm certain it can do the same for you. Gradually, as you read aloud, you'll begin to feel more comfortable; then you can make the transition between reading someone else's words and speaking – dictating – your own. Revelation! If you can KEEP TALKING, the battle is more than half won.

If you hesitate, don't lose confidence. Go back to reading aloud, another page or two, then try another time, and if necessary, still another. Sooner or later you'll succeed – that I guarantee.

NOTE: Even if you have a secretary who is extremely skilled at taking dictation, try using a dictating machine in doing these first exercises. When you become sufficiently fluent (and comfortable), that's time enough to start dictating live.

KEYWORD TWO – PATIENCE

Set aside a period each day – preferably at the same time – and practice at least 15 minutes. BE PATIENT. Don't give up. Let nothing interfere. What you are doing now is forming a habit: this time today – and EVERY working day – is dictation time.

For most of us, morning hours are best. But you know yourself better than I do. Pick your own time, then stick to it. You'll find that some days go much better than others. Before long, the worst days will be better than the best ones were when you started, just as when you were learning to write in longhand or to type.

KEYWORD THREE — PICTURES

Psychologists tell us that human beings think in terms of visual images. We translate these visual images into words, which are, after all, only symbols. Take advantage of this natural thinking process and use it to the fullest. PICTURE the person you are writing to, as clearly as imagination will permit. That's right — I want you to SEE that person sitting across from you and looking back with great interest. It's up to you to EARN that interest.

KEYWORD FOUR — PLAINTALK

Be conversational. Use common, ordinary, everyday words — PLAINTALK — that's what you want. It's amazing what you can do if you put your mind to it. So concentrate, tell yourself you can dictate like a professional. Then be ready for a pleasant surprise when you read the transcription back later. Particularly if some of your writing tends to be stiff, you'll be much easier, much more conversational, and that — believe me — is all to the good.

What a great feeling when you first discover how much better those words look on paper than you thought they would when you dictated them. (Nobody was ever more surprised than I was.)

Also, it's a continuing joy as each day the dictation begins turning out better and better. Of course, you may wonder how that can be, with your nitpicking inner critic turned off. Oh, that's just for getting started. Besides, that rascal is AL-WAYS on your back, once you begin editing the transcribed copy. All you've done is shunt the critical appraisal to the REWRITE phase, where it belongs in any case.

KEYWORD FIVE – PACE

Keep up a measured pace – not too slow, not too fast. Sort of "half fast," as Satchmo used to say. This means you don't need to try thinking too far ahead. Just a sentence at a time, or maybe two, as your powers increase. Practice by telling yourself stories, recounting the day's events, or updating old jokes.

Make sure to speak in complete sentences. Put in commas and periods and paragraphs. (We'll talk more about the mechanics of this later.) You can help your transcriber or secretary with appropriate punctuation, pauses, and special instructions, but right now it's a bit early to be concerned; don't worry about mechanics until you know for certain you are over your dictaphobia, once and for all.

Summing Up

There you are. The five P's, the five magic KEYWORDS. Faithfully use them for a few days, and you'll know when you're ready for the next step. Meanwhile, to aid your memory, here they are again:

1. PRACTICE. Read aloud if you must, to get started, but talk into that mike. Don't let that little thing scare you.

2. PATIENCE. Don't give up. Practice every day at the same time. Hang in there.

3. PICTURES. Keep a mental image of the person you're talking to clearly in your mind. The sharper your picture, the more fluent your dictation.

4. PLAINTALK. Make sure you sound like a human being, not a machine talking into a machine. Use everyday language anyone can understand. Gobbledygook is a dirty word.

5. PACE. Once your words are flowing, keep them going. Don't try to think too far ahead — a sentence at a time, or maybe two. It's okay to pause and collect your thoughts before you go on, but don't let your mind go fishing. The trick is to keep up the flow.

*I'll play it first
and tell you what it is later.*
— *Miles Davis*

5: For Dictators without Secretaries

You Are Not Alone

Many of my writer friends who reviewed early drafts of the original version of this book asked: "Why do you talk about dictating as if it's a skill only executives can use? Do you mean to imply that freelancers and others — perhaps those working in their homes — can't use dictation?"

The late Laura Horowitz waxed eloquent (which is better than waxing Roth, who doesn't like it at all): ". . . if you don't have a wife or secretary to transcribe and retype for you, where's the savings? Most writers can't afford secretaries — or are you arguing that they can?"

Her associate Peggy Smith took up the cudgels: "The text seems to be aimed entirely at executives who dictate letters to secretaries or recording machines. If I have no access to a secretary, how can the book help me? What student (or $20,000-a-year freelancer) can afford to dictate? What do transcribing services cost? Where are the Poggys?"

Their comments are (belatedly) well taken. I've already admitted my big mistake — namely, that when I dictated the first draft, I thought the book WAS just for executives. Indeed, the original title was *The Executive's Guide to Effective Dictation*. In spite of some pretty strong hints, like those just mentioned, it was only after the first edition was in print that the light really dawned: *dictation can be and should be for EVERYONE who writes.*

So that is why I'm writing this chapter specifically for those of us — and most of the time I consider myself a part of the group — who must be do-it-ourselfers. Let me assure you here and now that dictation can help folks like us, almost to the point of working a few miracles. But it does take a bit of effort, and more than a bit of ingenuity to make up for the lack of cash.

Commercial Transcribing Services

To start with, in most cities of any size at all, commercial transcribing services are available. You can find out who does what by letting your fingers do the walking. Look first under the heading *Secretarial Services*. If you don't find a listing there, you might try *Public Stenographers*, and if that fails, try *Typing Services* or perhaps *Editorial Services*.

Sooner or later you'll strike pay dirt. In my own area, for example — the Washington Metropolitan Area, there are several pages of listings under the heading *Secretarial Services*. As an experiment, I started at the top of the list and dialed each service, taking notes the while. Mostly I was trying to find out what such services cost and what the services included. I made some surprising discoveries.

For one thing, I was shocked at the prices. The last time I had checked, there were still a few organizations around that charged considerably less than a dollar a double-spaced page to transcribe, using a pica type machine (10 characters to the inch). Well, I hadn't allowed for inflation. Many of the persons I talked with would not even quote me a price by the page: they would give an hourly rate only. Incidentally, that rate ranged from about $10 an hour, which was the minimum quote I received, up to as much as $20 an hour.

I asked myself how I could possibly expect poor starving freelancers to pay that kind of money. Still, because I was not halfway through the exercise, I decided I had better go through the rest of the arithmetic.

For example, how much typing could a reasonably good transcriber be expected to turn out in an hour? (Surely it is safe to assume that anyone advertising in the Yellow Pages would be a reasonably good transcriber.) I didn't know, so I asked. Most of the professional transcribers said that if I sent them a one-hour cassette, it would take from three to four hours to transcribe it. Apparently that ratio is fairly standard in the business. So I got out my pocket calculator and found that, at 140 words a minute, it would take about two minutes of dictation to fill one page of typewriting. Thus, a one-hour cassette would convert into about 30 pages. At a rate of $15 per hour (it was $10 in 1980!) that 30 pages would cost from $30 to $40; or slightly more than a dollar a page. At the top rate quoted, $20 per hour, the rate would come out to more than $2.00 a page. (You can see that making a few calls for purposes of comparison would be well worth the time.)

The next question is, can you afford to pay that kind of money as a trade-off for saving a more than equivalent amount of your own time? Only you can answer that question. I know what my own answer would be: NO, a thousand times NO.

But if you can afford it, more power to you. This is undoubtedly the simplest, if not the cheapest, solution to your problem. If you are more like me, and decide you CAN'T afford it, fortunately there are alternatives. Let's consider a few:

Seek and Ye Shall Find

It is a fact of life that many persons with excellent secretarial skills are not employed—or at least not at full-time paying jobs. For one reason or another, these persons are unwilling or unable to put in eight hours a day. But many of them would be delighted to work for a shorter period daily or, occasionally, at times of their own convenience and choosing. If you can track down such a person, you may have the answer to your prayer.

A few inquiries, with minimal effort on my part, disclosed that there is probably an available and largely untapped market here; indications are that many capable persons, working at home and at odd hours, stand ready and able to transcribe your cassettes, at rates ranging somewhere between 50 cents and a dollar a page. All you have to do is find one.

The easiest and most obvious way would be to run a small classified *Help Wanted* ad. You may even get enough responses to be quite choosy.

Ina Lerner has suggested another way: call a local secretarial school, business school, or community college. Often they have students enrolled who would like to polish their skills, get some experience, and make a bit of money to help with the tuition.

Drawing from these sources, you stand a good chance of finding someone to transcribe your drafts for a dollar a page or less. Check this out — it's a good way to go.

Rolling Your Own

The cheapest way (in money, if not in time) to get your dictation transcribed is to learn to do it yourself. I can promise you that you won't enjoy it. As a matter of fact, by any stretch of the imagination, there is no way that you can call transcribing anything but a no-fun-at-all process. It is difficult and demanding work, and many persons who have chosen this masochistic calling feel unappreciated and improperly rewarded. On the other hand, several transcribers told me they loved their work and fussed at me for badmouthing it. Be that as it may, one of the interesting by-products of my calls to professional transcribers listed in the Yellow Pages was the discovery that one out of four had gone out of business. There may be some kind of a moral there.

It is precisely because good transcribing is difficult and unrewarding that I have written this book to teach you how to dictate better and more effectively. A good dictating technique unfortunately cannot make life easy for the transcriber — but it can make life *easier*, and that's better than nothing. I figure I should sell at least a million books or so to secretaries and transcribers who will want to give them to their bosses.

One way to dictate better is to listen critically to play-backs of your own recorded dictation. You already know the bad news about how hard the transcribing job is — check yourself to see if you are making it harder. The good news is that it is much easier for YOU to transcribe your OWN dictation than it is for an operator who is unfamiliar with your dictation techniques. You won't be confused or put off by your own voice, style, phrasing, and pronunciation as another person might be. Because you are already familiar with the material, you are not likely to be confused by any words you hear on the tape; you won't misunderstand or misconstrue sentences or phrases.

Once you experiment by playing back your own tapes and trying to transcribe them, you'll find it concentrates the mind wonderfully. (As Sam Johnson once remarked about the prospect of being hanged.) You will learn quickly how important it is to speak without mumbling, and to avoid breathing directly into the microphone. These miserable habits can be excruciating, and it's time you found that out personally. (One transcriber I know described the effect as sounding like someone giving birth to barbed wire.)

You'll also learn quickly how to speak in bite-sized phrases, with nice pauses between each phrase. Things go much faster when you can keep the tape rolling without constant backpedaling.

Dictation and Transcribing Machines—Get the Best You Can Afford

This information is extremely important. You won't believe ANYTHING in this book if I give you bad advice and you go out and buy dictating equipment that gives you only frustration. To preserve my credibility, I want you to get what is best for you—doing the job effectively and reliably, day in and day out.

You may be tempted (as I was) to take the apparently more economical course of simply buying a regular consumer-type cassette recorder. (In my case, I already had several.) I quickly found that most of these machines lacked the features I needed. I also learned that low-priced units tend to break down when subjected to heavy dictating use.

When I boned up on the subject by reading magazines such as *Office Product News*, I began to learn about new developments and features whose existence I hadn't even suspected. For example, even the tiniest portables now have goodies like a warning signal if the tape is about to run out. Even more valuable is the forward-reverse footpedal attachment that permits the transcriber to step on one side of the pedal to play the tape, and on the other side to back it up. A transcribing machine that has a variable-speed control is often helpful; this feature permits the operator to slow down the tape and decipher hard-to-understand words or phrases.

Going up the scale, more and more features are available. The fancier machines have ways of marking the beginning and end of each passage. They can also show the typist a clear indication of how much space each piece of typing will take, which saves time in arranging material properly on the page.

Some machines have a special editing feature that lets the dictator insert corrections right where they are needed (without erasing the original recording). Transcribers love this — it saves them from surprises. With the more elaborate machines, the refinements continue. I understand some of them can do almost everything — except maybe windows.

For maximum *recording* efficiency, you'd better give thought to getting a microcassette ultra-compact portable, small and light enough that you'll soon find yourself carrying it everywhere. Lou had one of these tiny marvels for months before I finally broke down and got one myself. In retrospect, that was one of my better decisions. Always having the machine there when I need it encourages me to use dictation more often, and more efficiently.

The Two-Recorder Technique

This next trick is strictly for freelance writers who can't afford the luxury of a secretary, and hence must transcribe all their copy themselves. It wouldn't be practical in a business office for many reasons too obvious to mention. The bad news is the expense — you have to buy **TWO** machines. First, one of the tiny portables I've previously mentioned; and second, a special transcribe-only machine to use for playback in the office.

I don't blame you for asking now, where is all the time-saving you've promised, if I must transcribe my own tape. Well, it is still there, but you just have to work at it a little harder. For one thing, the transcribing time can also be editing time. And frankly, I find the system I'm about to describe extremely effective.

(Again, what follows is a lightly edited transcription of my original dictation)

Having acquired the requisite two machines, I decided to experiment by using both of them at once. Now I use the technique frequently — mostly when I want to polish my dictation as thoroughly as possible **BEFORE** the transcribing stage. My routine usually goes something like this:

- I do almost all my initial, spontaneous dictation on the tiny portable machine, which I take with me almost everywhere, just as I have told you earlier. I find I can capture ideas as they come to me — ideas that might otherwise escape. I do this dictation at my normal speech rate. And since nobody will hear it but me, I don't worry about my technique — pauses, punctuation, or much of anything else except talking clearly and distinctly.

- When I get to my office, I put the recorded cassette on my fancy playback machine and play out a sentence at a time, using the foot-pedal. Meanwhile, I have the small portable in hand. I listen to each phrase or sentence from the original, edit it in my mind if that seems necessary or desirable, and re-dictate it on the portable, complete with the appropriate pauses, punctuation, and what-have-you.

- The net result is that before I ever get around to transcribing, I have essentially put the tape through an *initial editing*, cleaning up the worst messes, insofar as sentence structure, word choice, organization, etc., are concerned. It is amazing how much time this can save. The re-dictating goes quite quickly, and the transcribing in turn goes almost unbelievably faster, because I am systematically preparing the new version of the cassette in its optimum format.

Some Further Refinements of the Do-It-Yourself Approach

These ideas worked so well for me that I began to carry the refinements even further. Because transcribing is so painful, I decided that I would make the best possible use of *oral* techniques, with the idea of cutting down on the need for transcribing, typing, and re-typing. I started putting in one extra step, again a step that doesn't take long: play the tape through first to get the overall picture; *then* re-record. Somewhere along the way I found that sometimes it paid simply to listen through, then free-wheel a second version, before going to the "transcribing" format. *Save the lines that sing, kick out the rest.*

More Tricks for Tapping the Creative Levels of the Mind

And right along in here, my old friend Jim Aswell came to the rescue. About that time we were talking on the telephone a lot; Jim was living on the west coast and we hadn't seen each other face to face for more than 12 years, but we kept in close touch. I talked to him about this subject, and he thought things over and mailed me a cassette. I'll transcribe his exact words for you here:

> I took a certain amount of exception to what you had to say at the end of Chapter Four about "Don't let your mind go fishing." I know what you meant, and I agree in that context. But doggonit, when you get in a creative frame of mind, sometimes "going fishing" is one of the best things you can do. But you do have to keep up your nerve until you get used to the whole process.
>
> After dictating into a machine and playing back, your reaction could be one of appalled dismay. You might say to yourself, do I really talk that loosely? Do I ramble that much? Of course, when dictating a first draft a person tends to do this, unless you have an iron will and a sort of inhuman cohesiveness (that's not quite the word I want) to the outline you suggested they make. Just talking means that you get little side excursions, or you are not "talking." If you imagine you are talking to a friend (and I see you, old Jeff Bates, in three dimensions as I am talking to you now), all sorts of asides will come in.
>
> When you play back, until you get used to this, you may say, oh my, I'm going back to my sheaf of yellow paper and my old Oliver typewriter. (Oh, I'm sure there must be many Oliver typewriters in the executive offices of the government and the big corporations.)
>
> My point is, don't be disturbed to hear how loosely you talk. For, while you are doing that, fortunately, the ideas spring out of your brain that — in a puritanically disciplined use of handwriting or typewriting — would either not come to

mind at all, or would be discarded instantly as irrelevant or inappropriate. However, in the free working of the mind, sometimes things of shocking originality emerge; you are really astounded when you hear them. Hey, did I say that? That's pretty good. I'm going to use that.

So what you do, when you're creating, is to let your mind flow free; of course you'll have to edit and re-edit, and edit again. But if I know you, you would anyway. What was it you said in the self-editing chapter (Twelve) about the bleeding fingers?

Thanks, Jim. Old friend, you did it again. That's some of the best advice I ever received, and now I'm passing it on. I hope all you freelancers out there will hurry to your dictating machines and try Jim's system right away — as fast as you can. Because I am going to let you in on a little secret that I discovered a long time ago: Jim Aswell knew whereof he spoke — or dictated, as the case may be.

*My father sent me to engineering school
to prepare me for a literary career.*
— George Ade

6: Handling Correspondence —
Some Time-Saving Tips

Is This Dictation Necessary?

If you've read my book *Writing With Precision*, you already know that I advocate generating as little paperwork as possible; the best technique of all is to *speak directly* to the receiver of your message. Think of all the time and money that saves.

If you can't speak in person, *telephone*. And let's point out here that many of the techniques recommended for preparing to dictate can also be used for preparing to telephone with maximum efficiency. We'll talk more about that later.

But please don't get me wrong. Although oral communication is fast, efficient, useful, and direct, there are many cases when there is no substitute for writing. For accuracy, for a permanent record, for details of chapter and verse, the written word is still our best method. (For which I'm more than thankful — on the day writing becomes unnecessary, I'm out of business.)

Using 'Quick Response' Techniques

To hold the need for writing — OR dictation — to a minimum, many organizations use a special "quick response" printed form, with space for a message on the top half and room for the recipient to answer on the bottom of the same sheet. Such forms often come with a special carbonless second sheet attached. The recipient answers, tears off the second sheet for reference, and puts the original right back in the mail. This is a great time-saving device for all parties concerned; I recommend it heartily.

Short of this, the next best way of avoiding the need for dictation is to handwrite your response directly on the letter to be answered. Write the responses in the margins, or at the bottom of the page, and make a reproduction on a copying machine for files so you'll have a record of the entire transaction. Then return the annotated original to the sender. Neat, handy, and quick.

Unfortunately, in this less-than-perfect real world, your organization's supervisory echelon may not let you use this technique. Someone will probably dig up (or make up) an organization rulebook requiring you to answer correspondence by writing a new letter. In that case, don't fight city hall. Just use as much of the annotating technique as you can—which happens to be quite a lot.

Using a "Skeleton Outline"

Here's how: before you begin to dictate, pencil in the margin of the incoming correspondence a skeleton outline of your intended response— even a few words or phrases will help. Then, when you pick up the microphone or start to dictate to your secretary, use the notes as a springboard.

Some dictators highlight important items in a letter by using a high-lighter felt tip pen; others put marks along the margin to emphasize paragraphs or sentences they consider important. Either method—or perhaps some variation you design—will make your answers more effective; you'll quickly discover how they help you get straight to the point.

Another suggestion: as soon as you've made your notes on the correspondence and have your thoughts in line, dictate your answers immediately. Beware of the natural tendency to get to them at a "more convenient" time. Many management experts say the best trick of all is to get so organized that you handle each piece of correspondence only one time.

I agree — in principle. So far, I've never been able to do this consistently. For a long time I felt guilty about it; then I made an interesting discovery. Nobody else I know can do it, either. Probably the best any of us can do is to become aware of wasteful practices by making a checkmark on the corner of each item of correspondence each time we handle it. The accumulating checkmarks eventually become so embarrassing that the only way to save face is to take action.

Sorting Out Priorities

To save your time AND your secretary's time (if you have one), *organize* as much as you can before you start to dictate.

One simple and efficient way to tackle incoming mail is to divide it into four stacks, in order of priority:

Stack Number One requires no answer. If it contains information to be filed, so note. If not, toss it! The more you can toss, the better.

Stack Number Two requires an answer, but the answer may call for considerable research. You'll find it most efficient to postpone your response until you've been able to gather necessary facts.

Stack Number Three requires an answer, but you can assign it a low priority; no urgency is involved.

Stack Number Four is your top priority, requiring a quick response. You should start dictating your answers as soon as you are ready and able to do so.

Some of you may want to number your stacks in the other direction. Feel free. I've just told you the way I do it.

It occurs to me that some readers may take a dim view of sorting. Many executives would say — maybe you are one of them, and maybe you are right — that sorting should be left up to the secretary. That makes sense. I suspect I sacrifice efficiency because I enjoy sorting and reading my own mail. None of us is perfect.

Assigning Control Numbers

Although my former partner, Lou Hampton, is younger than I, he's been dictating longer. He started early and I didn't. When we were working together, he showed me many professional shortcuts I otherwise might have

had to discover the hard way. Or more likely, might not have discovered at all.

Lou said that one of the easiest and most useful techniques for handling incoming mail is to assign a *control number* to each letter. After the initial sorting to determine priorities, he lightly marks the upper righthand corner of each letter with a number combination made up of the month, the day of the month, and then /01, /02, and so on. Thus, the control numbers assigned on May 3 (of any year) might be: 5-3/01, 5-3/02, continuing in a descending order of priority. This ensures that the most important letters are answered first.

Using this system, instead of having to dictate the name and address of each individual, he can simply say:

"Letter Number 5-3/01 (followed by the appropriate dictation) . . . Sincerely, etc."

He follows this by leaving about five seconds of "dead air" (unrecorded space) on the tape, then says, "Letter Number 5-3/02," and continues.

The dictation completed, he gives the tape to the transcriber. With it goes a folder containing the letters, in order, with the circled control numbers on them. The transcriber pulls out a letter, compares the number with the number dictated onto the tape, then copies the name and address straight off the incoming letter.

NOTE: *One of the professional transcribers I interviewed says I must add a note of caution here. Since there is no backup plan to be sure the right response goes to the right person, the transcriber should ALWAYS check to make sure the response matches the sense of the incoming letter. Otherwise, a disaster COULD result!*

The system works. Furthermore, it's guaranteed to win your transcriber's or secretary's undying esteem. For saving both time AND trouble, it is truly a winner.

Using a Data Sheet

Another time-saver Lou suggested is the "data sheet" system. He keeps a writing pad handy; then, if he discovers that he needs certain information before he can answer a particular letter, he writes something like this on the data sheet:

"Letter Number 5-3/01 — Need company report for 1989, and names of new members of the board of directors . . . " or whatever.

He said you should be sure to spell out carefully just what data, what publication(s), or what other information you will need before you can answer the letter effectively. Then, simply assemble all the material listed on the data sheet and have the information lined up before you when you start dictating.

This technique prevents a lot of frustration. Experienced dictators know that once dictation begins, any interruption of the trend of thought — especially if the dictator must arise from the desk and go get a reference — will transmute that great flow of ideas into molasses.

With the data already in hand, you can look it over, get into a proper frame of mind, and dictate sentences that sound smooth, natural, and conversational. Even better, you'll know what you are talking about, and your words will show it.

Summing Up

The time-saving tips covered in this chapter are deceptively simple. Like many other basic things of this world, they possess one elegant quality: they work.

You'll regain all the time it costs you to learn them during the first week you apply them. Remember:

- Don't write — or dictate — at all if TALKING directly to the person involved will get the job done.
- If you can't talk directly, TELEPHONE.
- If a written response is required, use a "quick response" form if you can.
- If you can't use such a form, answer directly on the incoming letter unless your organization's policy forbids it.
- If you must dictate a response, ORGANIZE first — sort your mail by priority, assign control numbers, use a data sheet, and DICTATE!

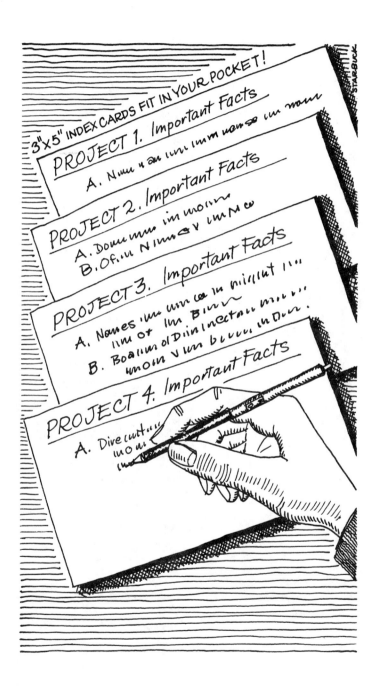

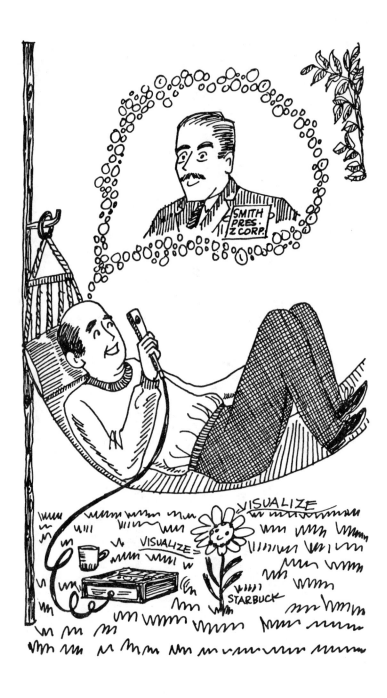

Before you try to tell the news,
Put yourself in your reader's shoes.
— Blessedly Anonymous

7: Audience Analysis — The Personal Touch

Know Your Reader

The difference between dictation that hits the mark and dictation that simply comes close — but not close enough — boils down to tailoring your message to appeal directly to your intended reader(s).

You can't expect to use the same approach for everyone. Allow for differences in background. Lou Hampton believes the secret of making dictation personal is to visualize the reader as a living, breathing human being.

If you know the person you're speaking to, visualizing isn't all that hard. Indeed, it should be downright easy; it doesn't take much imagination to talk to an old friend.

But what happens when you're answering a letter from someone you've never met? Then the problem is tougher — but not necessarily as tough as you might think at first.

Look for Clues

What do you need to know? And how are you going to find out?

Here's a checklist of some things you ought to look for if you intend to write a letter that really zeroes in on the reader:

Checklist for Audience Analysis:

- Occupation
- Educational background
- Level of experience
- Level of commitment/interest
- Age
- Sex

These are given roughly in order of importance; truthfully, the order doesn't make a lot of difference.

Be A Sherlock

Now that you know what information you're looking for, where are you going to get it?

The best clues can be found in the incoming letter. Study it: is it written on a professional letterhead? Or embossed or engraved personal stationery? Or is it on plain paper, or perhaps scrawled on a lined page ripped from a school tablet?

If it's on a letterhead, is the stationery custom designed, or is it the kind on sale at your friendly neighborhood Quick Print Shop? Can you tell anything from the firm name?

There's no intention of being snobbish here. I've used the friendly quick printer as often as anybody; the point is simply that you can often tell from these clues whether you're dealing with an individual, a small business, a multinational corporation, or whatever.

You'll also be better equipped to react appropriately if you know a person's occupation, job title, position in the company, or any other similar information. Even if you're called upon to furnish information to a school-child — as I often was when I was head of the correspondence branch at NASA — you'll respond better if you're aware of the whole picture.

Educational background and level of experience can often be determined by the content of the material in the letter. Of course, you can't *always* tell. Let me digress for a moment. You might even find it useful, and fun, to see if you can figure out whether a writer wrote or typed the letter personally, or had it done by a secretary. Sometimes it can be amusing to spot the tell-tale signs of a "personalized" letter that is mass produced by a computer or a word processing machine. For example, my publisher sometimes gets computer letters addressed to Mr. Acropolis Books Ltd. That's bad enough, but it gets worse when the computer takes the next step and addresses him as Mr. Ltd. at various spots throughout the body of the letter. Okay — enough of this — back to business.

How well are the ideas expressed? How about punctuation and grammar? Any misspelled words? All these items inevitably contribute to your overall impression, and hence to your answer.

Age may not seem important to you; however, it often meant a great deal to me when I was composing answers to incoming correspondence at NASA. Most of our young correspondents favored space exploration, so it was a pleasure for me to answer them. Many of the older ones, I'm sorry to say, were "a-gin' it."

Sex can usually, but not always, be determined by checking the person's name. Even if you are firmly convinced that sex should no longer be a consideration in the business world, it is useful to know — if only to help you figure out whether to say "Dear Ms." instead of "Dear Mr."

If the letter could have come from a person of either gender, one safe nonsexist solution is to write "Dear Lee Jones," assuming, of course, that the addressee's name is Lee Jones!

A Note On Alternative Salutations

While we're discussing salutations, let's face the fact that many persons undergo mental anguish trying to decide what salutation to use when the sex of the recipient is unknown. Standard practice in the old days was simply to write "Dear Sir," or "Gentlemen." Many writers today still do it — including, I find, many women. But others feel that this is grossly sexist, and won't do at all.

Some writers say "Dear Gentleperson." Maybe you find this solution satisfactory. Frankly, I don't. It sounds phony to me, so I usually go to a certain amount of trouble to avoid doing it that way.

I've seen letters with the salutation "Dear Sir or Madam," and that doesn't thrill me either. "Ladies and Gentlemen," seems to me to be a lot better.

Often a good way is to use a job title instead of a proper name. For example, "Dear Training Director," or "Dear Sales Manager," or even "Dear Colleague," assuming that the person addressed is indeed a colleague.

Lou suggests simply starting with a "Hello" or "Good Morning." Sometimes that works fine. "Greetings" would probably be okay if the sound didn't bring back so many unpleasant memories to those of us who once received a draft notice from good old Uncle Sam.

Finally, if you're still hung up, Casey Miller & Kate Swift have written a book called *The Handbook of Nonsexist Writing for Writers, Editors, and Speakers.* (New York: Lippincott & Crowell, 1980.) If that doesn't do it, we might as well all give up.

The *occupation* or profession is often self-evident from correspondence, or at least fairly easy to guess. Business executive? Lawyer? Physician? Accountant? Farmer? Engineer?

Taking a Second Look at Audience Considerations

Here's a good chance to work in a practical example. I'll risk being slightly repetitious, to make the point. As I have explained earlier, when I started work on this book, I was sure in my own mind exactly what the audience would be. *Too sure.* The original title of this opus reflected my misguided thinking. I was going to call it *The Executive's Guide to Effective Dictation.* As things turned out, that concept, and hence the title, was far too narrow. I still didn't have the complete picture, even in my own mind.

I saw the executive audience as divided into three groups: (a) executives and professionals who are already dictating, but would like to learn to do it better and more professionally; (b) beginners who would like to be instructed instead of having to learn dictation skills by trial and error; and (c) those who have always avoided dictating like the plague because of hang-ups.

I dictated the whole first draft aimed exclusively at this audience — and at nobody else. But (as I mentioned previously in Chapter Five) when I sent a copy of that draft to Laura Horowitz and her staff of writers, editors, and professional transcribers at Editorial Experts, Inc., their comments opened my eyes:

"Why should this be just for executives? How about writers, even those who don't have secretaries? How about students, or reporters, or teachers, or anyone who has to write anything at all? Don't they count?"

Who Needs to Learn Dictation Skills?

So my list of potential readers started to expand, and kept on expanding. Now it includes (and even this may not be a complete list):

- **actors**
- **disc jockeys**
- **editors**
- **engineers**
- **executives (all types, sizes, and descriptions)**
- **lawyers**
- **managers**
- **physicians**
- **public affairs officers**
- **public relations and advertising agency personnel**
- **public speakers**
- **reporters**
- **report writers**
- **salespersons**
- **scientists**
- **talk show hosts and participants**
- **telephone solicitors**
- **writers of every kind — fiction and nonfiction, poets, playwrights, novelists, speechwriters, ghostwriters**
- **and any others I may have accidentally omitted.**

A pretty impressive list. Dictation skills, obviously, are for almost everyone. So my book needed a new, broader approach, and even a new title. Back to the old dictating machine, one more time.

Dictating for the 'Average' Reader

From that example, I hope you can see how important audience considerations are, and how easily they can be misread. Now let's look at the problem from another angle: what if you don't have any really good clues about your reader or readers at all? What can you do then?

Well, while we can probably agree that there's no such thing as an "average" reader, it's still a handy fiction to suppose that such a reader does indeed exist. Certainly I've found it practical to maintain one in my own imagination during most of the years I've been writing for a living.

My average reader is practical and intelligent, but has not had special training in any particular discipline; hence, I automatically strive to avoid highly technical language or jargon. It goes without saying that if I must use a special term the reader might not know, I'll define it or add an explanation in lay language.

I give my reader credit for having plenty of good common sense, and enough pride to resent being "talked down to" or patronized in Dick-and-Jane sentences and word choices.

For my imaginary reader, I stick to simple, everyday words — most of the time. But I won't leave out what seems to be the perfect word choice for the occasion; furthermore, I'm not willing to sit idly by and let William Buckley and Henry Fairlie have *all* the fun. That's why in this book, perhaps in unexpected places, you'll sometimes run across polysyllabic curiosities such as *verisimilitude* and *omphaloskepsis* and *propaedeutical*. And I temper the long obscurities with an occasional short one. (Let's not take all the joy out of dictation; besides, maybe it will encourage you to get a new dictionary. Or, as my transcriber remarked to me somewhat caustically, "Maybe *you* will be searching for a new transcriber!")

What's In It For Me?

Remember the old saying, "What's in it for me?" (Sometimes abbreviated WIFM.) It's a key element in reader psychology.

What does your reader want or need from you? What desires are you prepared to fulfill, or to help fulfill?

What words or ideas can you dictate into your letter that will win a positive emotional response from your reader?

Again, what action are you trying to elicit FROM the reader? What can you say that will be most likely to achieve the desired response?

Sympathize and Empathize

Paint your own mental picture, so that you can see the reader as a real, live human being with likes and dislikes, loves and hates. Then put yourself into the shoes of the person you're addressing, and strive to follow the golden rule. This approach will just about guarantee that you'll be on the right track.

Anyway, you won't be on the wrong one. And in these parlous times, that's better than most of our politicians are doing.

Summing Up

Here's a brief recap on how to analyze (and slant for) your audience:

1. **Visualize your reader.** If you don't know the facts, look for clues.

2. **Try to determine the reader's occupation, educational background, level of commitment/interest, age, and sex.** All these items help establish your appropriate response.

3. **Use a salutation suitable to the reader's sex.** If that is unknown, try to find a nonsexist alternative salutation.

4. **Write for an "average reader" who is practical and intelligent, but has not had special training in any particular discipline.**

5. **Strive to fulfill the reader's needs.** RESPOND to the incoming letter.

*It is difficult to look farther ahead
than you can see.*
— Winston Churchill

8: Organizing for Dictation

Identifying Your Subject

Good organization is the wellspring of good dictation. This is so obvious I shouldn't have to say it. Obvious or not, say it I must — because many would-be dictators have never learned the basics, or (almost as bad) have forgotten what they once knew. Let's refresh our memories together.

The first step in any writing — and hence, in any dictating — is to *identify your subject.* Know exactly what you want to accomplish and you'll find that accomplishment much easier. Some years ago, Chuck Waterman made a speech about this before the Public Relations Society of America. He used a Norman Vincent Peale quotation that makes the point memorable: *"Write yourself a telegram."*

Chuck told his audience to write down, in not more than 20 words, a crisp statement of what the writing is all about. The "telegram" should set forth the aim exactly; this helps zero in on the best way to tackle the job.

Getting the Facts

The next step is to get the facts to make your points accurate — and BELIEVABLE. Jim Aswell used to say there is nothing like throwing in a few facts to give your message an aura of verisimilitude. Jim loved the sound of that word, even though it's just a fancy way of saying "give the impression you know what you're talking about."

If you need certain information you don't have, take the time to look it up. Don't fake it; the odds of your getting all the facts exactly right are strongly against you. If you are an executive, perhaps your secretary or a research aide will check things out for you. If you're a freelance writer, you already know you're going to have to do it yourself.

A practical approach for all us do-it-ourselfers is to use a card system. Because I majored in English and had to write essays and term papers by the dozen, I became hooked on using index cards while still an under-graduate student. A couple of years after the first edition of this book was published, I discovered the "perfect system" for handling and organizing index cards. It is called *Scan/Plan, The Creative Organizer.*[7] I have found the system so useful that I devoted almost an entire chapter to it in *The Portable Office.* It comes in different sizes and configurations, and I use them all, because they make up an integrated system. Each stands alone or works effectively with every other one in the system, saving a lot of duplicated effort.

My mainstay is the *Minipak*, which holds regular 3x5 index cards, not expensive off-sizes. The *Minipak* is small enough to carry in a pocket or purse, enabling researchers to keep important facts and figures neatly sorted out from the very beginning.

(If you collect trivia, you might be interested to know that great novelist Vladimir Nabokov is reported to have written many of his first drafts *entirely* on index cards.)

The Scan Page

The heart of the *Creative Organizer* system is the *Scan Page*, a row of overlapping clear vinyl card pockets, with a lip at the bottom of each pocket, front and back. The overlap permits you to see the front of the first (top)

---

7   For more information, write to Scan/Plan, The Creative Organizer, Post Office Box 1662, Santa Monica, CA 90406. Or call 1-800-SCANPLAN.

card, and the bottom lines of all the rest. Just flip up the first pocket and you can see the entire next card, as well as the back of the first one. In other words, each card is "flippable," so you can see both sides.

The flexibility of the *scan pages* immediately solved a problem that had plagued me for years: how to handle and organize effectively the stack of 3x5 cards, wrapped in rubber bands, that have habitually resided in my inside coat pocket. Now, when I take notes, things are a lot different from the "olden days"—all those oddball, nondescript, seemingly unrelated cards are neatly organized and fitted into *scan pages*. (I'll tell you more about how I use the system for big projects—such as books—in Chapter Fifteen.)

Selecting the Essentials

Somewhere along the way you'll have to select what is important and weed out what is unimportant. My philosophy is to keep all options open as long as possible. In particular, don't get lazy and skip putting down notes on your cards because you aren't entirely sure you are going to use them. That's tempting fate—and Aswell's Adjunct to Murphy's Law: *If you don't think you are going to need it, you undoubtedly will.*

Experience shows that too much information is a whole lot better than too little. A smidgen of extra care at this point may save an unwanted return trip to fill in blanks. What's more, the next time you may not be able to track down the information. (I fell victim to such carelessness when I neglected to note some figures on how many companies have installed expensive dictating equipment, only to have it go unused because they hadn't properly trained their employees to use it. I lost the reference and have never been able to find it again.)

Here, incidentally, is another great assignment for your portable cassette recorder. Supplement your cards by dictating auxiliary information; this cuts down your writing chore, while ensuring you'll have all the information you need. My old friend Pat Jones has used this technique for years.

After these admonitions about completeness, I probably sound like the Department of Anticlimax when I tell you to weed out every card not clearly related to the points you want to drive home. Once you begin to dictate—

and later, to write—deciding what *not* to use is fully as important as deciding what *to* use.

Making a Scratch Outline

Once you have all the facts, you're ready to make a scratch outline. For short pieces of writing such as letters and memos, a simple "laundry list" is all you need. For longer pieces, such as speeches, reports, or books, you'll have to make an outline that's a good deal more elaborate. Don't worry about that now—we'll cover that subject in detail later in the book.

Many proficient dictators I've interviewed make scratch outlines on a legal pad. That's an okay method, but frankly, I don't think it's the best one. For uniformity, as the years go by, I am more than ever persuaded that *the best possible way to make an outline is to list each point on a separate index card.* Then lay out the cards and shuffle them around until you achieve the most logical order. This is much more flexible than using a legal pad, even for short jobs. (It's so easy to reshuffle the cards and come up with a brand new outline if the old one doesn't track right!)

The only other tool you need at this point is a well-sharpened pencil (fairly soft—Jim Aswell used to go to a lot of trouble to get a 1½. I willingly settle for a No. 2) or an easy-writing pen. If your writing instrument requires heavy pressure, or won't make a neat, crisp line, you may get so frustrated that your thought processes won't flow properly either.

Okay, you're ready to begin. Here's a step-by-step breakdown:

1. Write the statement of purpose (the telegram to yourself).

2. Write down the main points you want to include: put just one item on each line, leaving a couple of spaces between lines. (Or use separate slips or cards, one per item, if that's the system you have chosen.)

3. When you've finished writing down every point you can think of, stop and let your mind absorb the total problem. Relax, take a deep breath, and look at the list as if you had never seen it before. Imagine yourself as the intended reader. What items on the list would seem most important to you?

4. Assign the numerical priorities. That sounds fancy in these words, but it's simple. Just spread your cards out in such a way that you can look at the whole list. Then arrange them in a logical order.

A good principle to follow is *(a) to start with the known — something the reader is familiar with — and move a step at a time to the new or unknown* material; or *(b) to start with the general or more widely applicable items, and move a step at a time, narrowing things down more and more specifically.*

For an object lesson in how to do this, try reading almost any nonfiction by Dr. Isaac Asimov. (He doesn't need my recommendation, but he happens to be one of the all-time masters of explaining difficult concepts in simple language.)

Just now, choosing at random, I pulled from my shelves an Asimov book on the physical sciences. It begins with a chapter on "What Is Science?" and the opening paragraph consists of a single line: "Almost in the beginning was curiosity."

From that lead, guaranteed to make you keep on reading, Asimov goes on to explain that living organisms are curious and dead matter is not. We already know that — so it is familiar. But the approach gets us thinking as he gradually — one easy step at a time — presents his premise: the more advanced the brain, the greater the curiosity.

Keeping Your Options Open

Dr. Asimov interrupted my work for almost an hour; when I looked up that example I got hooked. Now I must get back to dictating more about the beauties of the free-wheeling, informal card system outline.

The best thing about using index cards is that the system lets you keep your options open as long as possible. I took advantage of this flexibility in organizing this book, which changed shape a number of times as I dug more deeply into the writing and editing processes. Some material originally intended to appear in early chapters was shifted, and much material within individual chapters was pushed around until it all tracked.[8]

---

8 As you may have suspected, the first chapter originally dictated was Chapter Four, at the time intended to be the introduction. Now, with this new edition, I've added two more chapters and other new material, and plugged everything in at appropriate places. Fortunately, the *Scan/Plan* system made this major overhaul much easier for me to visualize.

NOTE: *As I mentioned earlier, the outlining process used for this book is somewhat more elaborate than the simple scratch outline discussed in this chapter. I give a full breakdown in Chapter Fifteen.*

The creative mind works in a mysterious way. No outline made in exact detail in advance of the actual dictation or writing is likely to be satisfactory in every respect. Sometimes it won't work at all. As a writer tackles the problem head on and starts to dictate, the subconscious mind inevitably goes to work; quite often, it takes control and comes up with a better way.

Thus, the trick is to keep yourself from getting locked into a rigid format too early. If you discover during dictation that your mind balks at a particular approach, that may be a signal that your logic is faulty. Remind yourself that your outline isn't set in concrete. Fall back and regroup; take a second look. Then, if it seems advantageous to do so, shuffle the deck and deal a new hand.

Dictating the First Draft

Once you're reasonably satisfied with your scratch outline, put it to work by using it as a skeleton. To explain this step clearly, if inelegantly, what you must do is *hang the meat on the bones.*

Study your statement of purpose and compose an opening sentence or a very short paragraph that is a real grabber. As an example, let's assume you're going to dictate a letter to the executive board of your company, setting forth your recommendations on management objectives for the coming year.

Do you have a new product? A new market? A technique to increase profits? These are the kinds of ideas that inspire your readers to keep on reading.

As important as the lead itself is the position you take concerning it. If your letter is going to accomplish its intended purpose, you must take a definite stance and make it known to your readers as early as possible. You are not writing a detective story; keeping readers in suspense is out.

Get your dictation rolling. Don't struggle too long about exact wording when dictating the lead — just make sure you state it clearly. Polish up the language during the editing phase, after the first draft has been completed, and — if possible — given a chance to cool for a while.

Establishing Credibility

If you are writing a letter to readers who already know you well, you can ignore the step of "establishing credibility." But if you are an unknown quantity to them, you should make your credentials known — as early in the writing as possible, show your special knowledge, your expertise. Do this as modestly and unobtrusively as possible, but do it! Prove to the reader that your opinions are worth reading and heeding.

This book might be a good example, since I had two strikes against me when I started. Not only did I not have a reputation as an expert on dictation, but many of my colleagues knew at first hand that I was a dictaphobe. To overcome that handicap, what could be a more convincing demonstration, or better evidence, than to *dictate* a book on dictation?

Remember that the entire purpose, whether or not we are consciously aware of it, is to *convince* readers. To SELL a point of view, the writer must establish credibility in every possible way.

Arranging for Maximum Impact

How do you arrange arguments for maximum impact?

There are at least two major schools of thought on this subject. Pick the one you are most comfortable with.

METHOD ONE is to lead off with your strongest point: assume that you are going to use a total of three points, which, incidentally, happens to be a good number. Follow with your weakest argument in the second position, and close with the next-to-strongest argument. (Lou Hampton casts his vote for this method.)

METHOD TWO draws on the technique a good debater might use. Begin with a strong argument, but not the best one. As before, follow with a weaker argument. (In the "three point" case, the weakest argument would come in second position.) Close out with your blockbuster — the strongest argument of all. BUT — make sure you've brought the reader along with you all the way. Be brief, be forceful, and take care not to drag in any extraneous ideas. Above all, don't let the reader's attention lag.

After the final point, remember to do what any good salesperson must always do: **ask for the order!** That is, ask for action. If you're trying to get someone to vote for a cause you believe in, ASK for that vote. If you want your boss to accept a course of action, **recommend it!** Close on your strongest note.

This approach works for almost any kind of letter, not just a sales letter. It works best if you can infuse some honest emotion into your dictation. Believe in what you are saying. If you don't, you'll get the effect Sam Clemens ("Mark Twain") was talking about when his wife tried to shame him into deleting some expletives.

Sam sang out a few ringing Anglo-Saxon monosyllables. Then his lovely, sedate wife, a "preacher's kid," repeated his exact words right back at him.

"Livy," Sam said affectionately, "you've got the words, but you haven't got the tune!"

Make sure you've got the tune.

SUMMING UP

For your convenience, here are the high points of how to organize for dictation:

1. **Identify your subject.** "Write yourself a telegram."

2. **Get the facts** — use a card system; augment your written notes with your dictation machine.

3. **Select the essentials; weed out the rest.**

4. **Make a scratch outline.**

5. **Keep your options open.** if your outline isn't logical, re-order it and try again.

6. **Hang the meat on the bones by using the outline as a skeleton.** Start with a "grabber" that will get the reader's attention.

7. **Establish credibility by showing your special knowledge or expertise.**

8. **Arrange your presentation for maximum impact** on the reader.

9. **Close on your strongest note.** Ask for action.

*That man's silence
is wonderful to listen to.
— Thomas Hardy*

9: The Mechanics of Dictating

Secretaries Are Human, Too!

Someone has to transcribe your golden words, whether you dictate into a machine or speak directly to a secretary or stenographer. So now it's time to talk about techniques to make the transcription as easy and painless as possible. Unfortunately, these are things that many dictators — even some who have been at it for a long time — have never bothered to learn.

In researching for this chapter, I've interviewed most of the good dictators I know. Perhaps more important, I've interviewed their secretaries or transcribers (a most revealing experience).

I've augmented this information from my own experiments, including some things I've learned to do right only because I first did them wrong. Some of the most practical discoveries stem from the fact that my wife, Poggy, who volunteered to transcribe this book, has given me the straight scoop, unrestrained by the inhibitions of a secretary. (That may be the understatement of the year.)

Poggy really deserves more than my standard remark about owing her more than I ever can repay. (Which, of course, I do.) She has often proofed, looked things up, and helped me in many other ways in the past, but this is the first time she transcribed from tape. She volunteered to learn this new skill just to be my guinea pig as well as my helpmeet. I admire her courage.

Learning From Mistakes

Until Poggy and I began this experiment, I was simply unaware of many typical beginner's mistakes in dictating techniques. Of course, an experienced secretary/stenographer can compensate for a multitude of sins; that's why I wanted to test my theories with someone new to transcribing.

When Poggy started learning the deceptively simple-looking skills of the foot pedal, for example, she was preoccupied with the mechanics of playing back the tape; her lack of experience put a bright spotlight on some of my more obvious errors as a dictator—mostly sins of omission in not specifying special instructions properly. Just look at the sample page of typed transcription I'm using here as an illustration, and I think you'll see right away what I'm talking about.

My fatal error was that I interspersed some instructions along with the straight typing without giving her a clear indication of the difference—you can see what happened. This really drove home to me how important it is to "label" special instructions clearly.

```
    Good morning, Poggy. This is the morning of
November 29, 1979, and this dictation is for
Chapter Two of the dictation book. I want you
to put this quotation at the top righthand
corner of the page. Quote. My father sent me
to an engineering school to prepare me for a
literary career. End quote and go down two
spaces. Dash, George Ade. Now go down a
couple more spaces and put Chapter Two at
```

left margin. Now go down a couple more spaces
and put in the subhead, Is This Dictation
Necessary? Then go down another double space
and indent for paragraph.

If you've read my book underscored Writing
With Precision, you already know I advocate
generating as little paper work as possible.
Best trick for answering incoming correspondence that I've seen yet is simply to make
handwritten responses right onto the letter
itself. Make your response semicolon run off
a copy for your files semicolon send the
original back, and the sender has the question and the answer, or whatever it may be,
right there handy in one piece period new
paragraph.

All this seems simple, in retrospect. (Poggy says many things seem simple in retrospect.)

Anyway, after much trial and error, and dozens of interviews with skilled dictators, secretaries, and transcribers, I finally came up with the information I am now setting forth for you on the pages that follow, as the **Twelve Commandments of Good Dictation.** The first three apply BEFORE you begin to dictate. The other nine involve the actual dictation process. Here goes:

THE TWELVE COMMANDMENTS OF GOOD DICTATION

COMMANDMENT I. ORGANIZE.

Before you pick up the microphone or call in the secretary, get ready. Think. Remember the basics you've learned in the earlier chapters.

COMMANDMENT II. GET YOURSELF IN THE DICTATING FRAME OF MIND.

To do a good job, it's important to psych yourself up, almost the way an actor prepares to go onstage for a performance. (You might find it helpful to read about the psychology of the creative process. I recommend *The Act of Creation*, by Arthur Koestler. See *Bibliography*.)

COMMANDMENT III. DICTATE IN ORDER OF PRIORITY.

Using the control number system described in Chapter Five, it's a simple matter to put the most important items at the beginning. (Many dictators don't; instead they put in a hodgepodge of priority instructions right on the tape, sometimes in very odd places. I'm surprised their secretaries don't shoot them.)

COMMANDMENT IV. IDENTIFY YOURSELF, AND GIVE DATE AND TIME OF DICTATION.

Always identify yourself at the beginning of the tape. *(A transcriber commented: "I like it when the dictator starts a new tape with a little bit of warmth and humanity. Even saying, 'Good morning, operator,' or better still, addressing the transcriber by name — can make a difference.")*

Depending on the size of your organization, or how many other persons must share your secretary, transcriber, typing pool, or word processing group, give as much information as necessary to make identification quick and easy. This could include your job title, department, an office or correspondence symbol, or telephone number. Give only as much of this information as is needed for identification and ease of processing — no more.

Put in the date and time of the dictation. (You'd probably be horrified to know how many times a tape has been mistakenly re-transcribed under the misapprehension that it's new dictation, just because a cassette has been improperly labeled or identified.)

COMMANDMENT V. SPECIFY INSTRUCTIONS.

Identify each one clearly as an instruction. A useful technique is to say preferably in a different tone of voice: "Instruction." **Or speak to the secretary or transcriber by name.** The point is, make the instruction CLEARLY different and distinguishable from the dictation proper. If you are musically inclined you might (as does one pixie-ish fellow I know) hum the opening notes of Beethoven's Fifth; just make sure your transcriber is aware that this is your special signal for an instruction. On the other hand, if you have a tin ear or a tinnier voice, your off-key endeavors may inspire revenge. Perhaps it would be safer just to say "Instruction."

Identify each item as a memo, letter, report, etc., as appropriate. If special paper, letterhead, or plain bond should be used, say so early in your instructions. **Very early!** Also give any necessary information on number of copies, distribution, enclosures, and so on. You might want to tell how long (approximately) a given item is going to be. If you want it done in rough draft first, say so. (While you're learning, I hope you'll *always* ask for a rough draft first. With today's word processors, this is no big deal. I know some self-styled experts who want to go straight to the final form. I'll guarantee you one thing: on anything I consider important, I never will. The savings are minimal, and the chances for embarrassment are substantial.)

COMMANDMENT VI. SPEAK CLEARLY.

If you are dictating live, face the secretary and don't mumble into your fist. **Enunciate.**

(**NOTE:** *A transcriber reviewing these commandments said here, "You have reduced the whole process to one word. Almost everything will fall into place if there is no question regarding the spoken word."*)

Dictators often get so carried away with the spirit of the dictation that they fail to pronounce words carefully or to realize that some words may be unfamiliar to the transcriber. Another caution; don't gnaw on a cigar, bite your pencil, or chew gum while you talk.

If you use a dictating machine, do not talk directly into the mike. Speak ACROSS it, and keep a few inches of distance between it and your lips. For most persons, about four to eight inches is optimum, but you can test quickly by saying a sentence or two at different distances, playing back, and listening carefully to your voice quality and the clarity of the reproduction. Above all, try not to breathe straight into the mike. This is rough on the transcriber, because the sound of the breath is exaggerated and can be very annoying on playback. Transcribing from tape is a demanding and wearying job, particularly if the transcriber must wear the earphones for long periods. The sound of raspy breathing can become almost unbearable, so don't make the time seem even longer than it is.

COMMANDMENT VII.   PACE YOURSELF.

Don't dictate too fast OR too slow. If you are dictating live, you can quickly tell when your secretary is being thrown off by your rate of delivery. With a machine, you can talk at pretty much your normal speed IF you phrase in such a way that the transcriber can get the sense of your words without constantly having to back up the tape.

The average transcriber can play and comprehend roughly 15 to 25 words at each forward "pedal." That is, the transcriber will depress the foot-pedal, listen to a comfortable amount of words, type that much of the sentence, and then start the tape forward with the pedal again. If your dictation is poorly phrased or enunciated, the transcriber must backpedal and play the same portion of the tape again. This fault is relatively harmless if it happens only occasionally, but it can be totally frustrating if it occurs in every sentence. The trick of the true professional is to phrase so the operator can keep an unbroken rhythm. Then the work will go remarkably fast.

COMMANDMENT VIII. PAUSE.

When it is appropriate to do so, pause. With live dictation, your secretary can help you and you'll probably learn quickly. With a machine, you may not unless you think about it consciously and conscientiously. Your recorder, depending on how elaborate it is, may have a simple one-button control that does everything, or it may have a separate PAUSE button. Use the pause control judiciously. If you are using even the most inexpensive cassette recorder, you can get a mike equipped with a start-stop switch; that way, you can leave the machine in RECORD mode throughout your dictation, and start and stop action from the mike control.

If you check yourself out by listening to some of your own tapes, maybe this practice will help you get the hang of the well-timed pause. You'll probably find that problems arise not so much because you dictate too fast, but because you aren't phrasing — and pausing — properly.

Once you master the art of putting a pause of the right length after each sentence or long phrase, you may achieve the ideal. At just the right combination of speed, timing, phrasing, and pausing, the transcriber can put the pedal to the metal, as CB-ers used to say.

If you find yourself at a temporary loss for words, don't let the tape keep rolling. A long stretch of "dead air" (unrecorded tape) seems interminable to the transcriber, and can add to frustration. Think what those eighteen-and-a-half minutes did to Rosemary Woods. Use the PAUSE control, think of what you're going to say next, and then continue. There will be only a slight amount of dead air on the tape.

COMMANDMENT IX . SPELL THINGS OUT.

Spell things out when necessary, and that is more often than you might think. If you use an unusual word, or a word that sounds like another one with which it might be confused, say "I spell," and spell it out. (**NOTE:** If any of the letters you spell out sound similar — for example, "m" and "n", or "b" and "p", use the *phonetic alphabet,* shown in *Appendix A* of this book.)

Lou Hampton has always said to take nothing for granted; spell out, for example, *every* proper name, even an apparently common one: *Wolf, Woolf, Wolfe; Smith, Smythe; Jon, John;* and so on. Lou tells of several cases where he had assumed the name was common and it came back with an alternative spelling he'd forgotten about while dictating. (**NOTE:** *A transcriber commented: "This is REALLY important. However, if the name is on the attached incoming correspondence, the dictator can refer to the transcriber to that, instead of spelling out the name."*)

COMMANDMENT X. PUNCTUATE.

Depending on how familiar you are with the abilities of the secretary or transcriber, you may see fit to specify more or less punctuation. Many good transcribers tell me they dislike having dictators put in more punctuation than they need; they assure me they can tell when commas are required, for example, from phrasing — assuming that the dictator is reasonably good at phrasing! But almost **all** transcribers appreciate your putting in such punctuation marks as parentheses, colons, semicolons, question marks, quotation marks (single and double), hyphens, dashes, and periods. (Indeed, **especially** periods.) Indicate the end of a paragraph by saying "Period. New paragraph." (**NOTE:** *A transcriber commented* here: *"Run-on sentences are a transcriber's nightmare. Every dictator should make it a point to learn correct punctuation.")*

COMMANDMENT XI. SPECIFY THE END.

Specify the end of each message. Many machines have a device that does this electronically; if not, just say "End of Message 6-12/01" and leave a few seconds of dead air. Then start the next one with its control number. Specify the end of the day's dictation by saying, "End of dictation for May 6, 1990."

This is an apparently small thing, but it's important — saving the transcriber from a time-wasting search through the rest of a tape. Even more important, it serves to keep the transcriber from missing some items because you left too much dead air between messages, leading to the assumption of "nothing more on this tape." (**NOTE:** *A transcriber commented: "It doesn't cost anything to thank the operator at the end of the tape — why not be really big hearted and say, "Have a nice day!"*)

XII. EDIT YOUR COPY.

Most careful dictators have learned the hard way that it's good practice to check a rough draft of the original dictation before going to final typing. Have the draft done in double or triple space. (Why is it so many typewriters and word processors nowadays don't have triple spacing?) You should have plenty of room to mark up the copy and make additions and corrections. This is your chance to get rid of overlong sentences, faulty constructions, bad grammar, and other crimes against the language and the reader. Clean it up. Be ruthless.

Comments from the Experts

I checked these Twelve Commandments out for myself in as many ways as I could think of. Poggy did the same. Then I consulted my panel of experts for their comments. (Some of the more cogent suggestions from transcribers were included as notes. Now I'll give equal time to the experts on the other side of the dictation process.)

Mostly, they agreed with my general premises. But they made some valuable comments. Let me recount some of them for you:

Chuck Waterman said I showed a definite bias in favor of machines over live dictation. He's right; I strongly believe that *dictating to a machine is far more time-efficient than tying up two persons using the "old fashioned" method of calling in a secretary or stenographer from other duties at a time chosen solely for the convenience of the boss.* Using the machine method, both parties are able to employ their time to maximum advantage. But fair's fair, so I had better put the opposing comments here:

Chuck reminded me: "Somewhere in the book I hope you'll acknowledge that a good secretary can be a tremendous help by asking questions as you dictate, prodding your failing memory, and providing words at points that the dumb machine won't be able to come up with."

Carl Sieg said, "Amen to that. Sometimes the best clue that your words aren't as well chosen as you thought comes when your secretary stops you and says, 'Are you sure you really mean that'?"

Okay, I've told their side. Fair's fair. But I reserve the right to the last word: *Machine dictation is far more efficient than direct dictation in time and convenience — both for the dictator and the secretary.*

Summing Up

For your convenience, I'm summarizing the Twelve Commandments here:

      I. ORGANIZE.

     II. GET YOURSELF IN A DICTATING FRAME OF MIND

    III. DICTATE IN ORDER OF PRIORITY.

    IV. IDENTIFY YOURSELF.

     V. SPECIFY INSTRUCTIONS.

    VI. SPEAK CLEARLY.

   VII. PACE YOURSELF.

VIII. PAUSE . . . when it is appropriate to do so.

    IX. SPELL THINGS OUT.

     X. PUNCTUATE.

    XI. SPECIFY THE END.

   XII. EDIT YOUR COPY.

*If at first you don't succeed,
you're running about average.
— Robert Orben*

10: How to Dictate Effective Letters and Memos

The Four Reasons for Communication

"In the business world," says Carl Sieg, "there are usually four main reasons for communicating: (1) to get information; (2) to give information; (3) to get action; and (4) to affect attitudes — that is, to make a friend."

Carl says he believes those AT&T ads we see on the tube: telephoning, even by long distance, is often cheaper and more effective than writing. I agree, but not strongly enough to suit Carl, who doesn't believe in half measures. He makes it a point that the techniques of effective dictation can be used, with little or no change, for effective telephone communication. He has even suggested that this book should have a chapter devoted to using the telephone effectively. He's probably right — usually is — but if I keep adding more chapters, I'll never finish. (Maybe one of these days Carl will write that book on effective use of the telephone himself. I hope so — can't wait to read it.)

Inevitably, the time comes when written communication is necessary — when accuracy is important, when legal or contractual matters are involved, or for some other good reason. Unfortunately, my experience indicates that much writing serves little purpose except to waste paper and clutter up the files. That's right—you know as well as I do that file cabinets everywhere are crammed with "memos for the record" obviously written for one purpose only—familiarly expressed in the abbreviation "C-Y-A." My euphemistic generation prefers to translate this as "Cover Your Anatomy."

Younger generations, I find, are more plainspoken.

How often are these memos necessary, really? I suspect 90 percent of them are overkill. Even so, I've C-M-A'd many times myself, and I'm certainly not going to advise you to skip it any time you have any doubts.

The word "memos" is, of course, the shortened form of the fancier terms "memorandums" or "memoranda." Hardly anyone uses the longer forms any more; also, saying "memos" gets us out of the bind of choosing between the alternatives.

Memos are usually reserved for internal communications. Except for that, there are few restrictions on their scope. To learn the accepted format within your organization, simply glance through the reading files.

The trouble with many memos is that they are overly formal and stuffy. Unless your organization's top management consists entirely of stuffed shirts, strict formality is usually unnecessary; besides, it's likely to interfere with the clarity of the communication. Things go much better with relaxed language; frequent use of the personal touch, addressing the recipient by name, or nickname, is good. Within the limits of good taste, slang and jargon are acceptable; ordinarily, profanity and obscenity are not.

Other than that, you don't need any special instructions for writing memos. The material on letters that follows generally applies to memos too.

How to Dictate 'Good News' Letters

Because you have been reading and writing letters all your life, you already know a great deal about the subject; it would be a waste of your time and mine to start at rock bottom here. If you consider this statement a copout, and sincerely want to know more about the *basics* of letter writing, check the bibliography at the back of this book. A few of the references listed there should give you all the confidence you need.

Here, since we are skipping basics, I'll begin with a subject that is one of the easiest to write letters about — the "good news" letter, as it is often called in books on business correspondence.

If you can dictate *any* kind of letter easily, a "good news" letter is undoubtedly the one.

The first thing to remember is *to get straight to the point.* With good news, that approach comes naturally. All you need know is that keeping the reader in suspense is "dirty pool." Don't impose an unduly long wait by putting in paragraphs of extraneous information. Tell the reader right up front that the check is in the mail, or the long-awaited promotion is approved, or the replacement parts for the 1931 Pierce Arrow are in stock.

Be sincere. Be gracious. Be human. As Mona Sheppard says in her excellent book, *Plain Letters,* "Use words that stand for human beings, like the names of persons and the personal pronouns *you, he, she, we,* and so on."

She goes on to say:

> In the first place, we muffle the tone of our sincerity by making our letters completely impersonal. We speak of *claimants, applicants, veterans,* and *suppliers*, when we might say *you, he, she,* or *Mr. Jones.* Instead of saying *you must apply by June 30*, we are inclined to say *persons interested in the position must file application by June 30.* Having divested our reader of his personality, we remove ourselves from the scene by avoiding the pronouns *I* and *we* as if we ourselves were not people. We refer to ourselves as *this Board, this department,* or *this agency* and write with the impersonal pronouns (*it will be appreciated, it will be understood*) as if we were machines . . . .

For that human touch every reader likes, use these words (personal pronouns, proper names, names that stand for human beings) whenever it is fitting to do so, remembering that the pronoun *you* is probably the most important word in any letter.

Mona Sheppard's advice applies to all kinds of letters, not just the good news variety. Indeed, her entire book, *Managing Correspondence: Plain Letters*, remains a classic of its kind. It is available from the Superintendent of Documents, U.S. Government Printing Office, Washington, DC 20401. When I first ran across this small masterpiece back in 1956, it cost 35 cents. Now it's $5.00. So much for progress — but it's still a sound investment.

How to Dictate 'Bad News' Letters

Most of us have a hard time writing a "bad news" letter. Maybe it is because we know Shakespeare was right when he said, "The nature of bad news infects the teller." He was referring, of course, to the pleasant old custom of putting to death the messenger who carried the bad news.

Fortunately, that custom these days, at least literally, "is more honored in the breach than in the observance." Just remember that when you have to tell readers any kind of news they'd rather not hear, what you usually *don't* want to do is get straight to the point. Use what is described in the King James version as "the soft answer that turneth away wrath."

Think up an innocuous opening intended solely to serve as a buffer — something to soften the blow and ease the pain of the bad news that must follow.

After the anesthetic, start a new paragraph in which you begin explaining and analyzing the overall situation. One device you might want to try is to hint at the bad news, but continue to withhold the worst part of it by "breaking it gradually." The jokes that are so popular these days; about "the good news and the bad news" are based on sound psychology. Most readers — except for the pessimistic few who would rather think the glass is half empty instead of half full — appreciate a writer's effort to put the best light on things.

But we can't put off delivering the bad news forever. When the time comes, Lou Hampton says a good device is to "sandwich" the bad news so it doesn't have to stand alone. If it is necessary to say "No" to one thing, try saying "Yes" to something else. Offer an alternative or alternatives if you can; then end with the friendliest tone possible under the circumstances.

My friend Jim Jeffries, who knows more about personnel management in a minute than Lou and I do in a year, adds a caution here. Says Jim: "there are times when the 'buffer' devices or 'sandwiching' methods are totally inappropriate. For example, suppose you have the unpleasant duty of reprimanding an employee. If you sandwich that reprimand between a couple of compliments, you may be surprised to find that the message you intended to *send* is not the one the employee *receives*. Take special care not to let that happen."

Jim gave me several other examples in which it would be totally inappropriate to begin with any trumped-up good news. If we put ourselves in the reader's shoes, Jim points out, how would we react to a letter worded like the one shown below?

```
Dear Cousin,

    The weather out here in California is beautiful. The

sun is shining and there isn't a cloud in the sky. We

certainly wish you could be out here with us to enjoy

it.

    Oh, by the way, our favorite Aunt Minnie died yester-

day . . . .
```

I think you'll agree that Jim has made his point!

Along with his words of caution, I'll add a few more of my own. When you find it necessary to apologize in a letter, do it graciously but succinctly. *Don't overdo it!* Be courteous without being obsequious. If you have done a good job of explaining, the apology should be unnecessary; instead of soothing the pain, what it may do instead is open a new barrel of snakes, and that's even worse than a can of worms.

Using the Positive Approach

As you close, reassure the reader — assuming that you can do so truthfully — that you do not deal exclusively in turndowns and negatives. Offer the possibility of "better luck next time," if that prospect is real. if it isn't, let well enough alone. Don't promise what you can't deliver.

Note that it's possible to say most things in at least two different ways — that is, with either a positive or a negative connotation. Many times a relatively minor change in language or sentence structure can make an amazing difference in the reader's reaction.

Practice using the more positive approach even when you must give an essentially negative message. For example, which one of these versions would be more likely to sit well with you if *you* were a disgruntled customer?

NEGATIVE. *We refuse to make any adjustment until you have returned the equipment you allege is faulty, and prove that you bought it on the date you indicate by sending a copy of the sales receipt . . . .*

POSITIVE. *We will be happy to make a prompt adjustment if you will return the equipment so our engineering department can verify that the performance is faulty. To help keep the records straight, please send a copy of your sales receipt along with the equipment, so we can check the guarantee and your date of purchase . . . .*

Surely you'll agree that the more positive response stands a better chance of keeping the goodwill of the customer — and that's the name of the game.

Keep your own "cool" and make it easy for all your readers to keep theirs. Dictating answers that will accomplish this isn't easy, but it isn't as tough as some persons appear to believe.

I'm sure most of the persons who upset their readers do it unwittingly. (If they intend to do it, that's something else entirely!) But what I am primarily talking about is the *"Who, me?"* attitude. They don't seem to realize that they are using a response almost guaranteed to irritate readers to the point of apoplexy.

How? By passing the buck — pretending that the problem either does not exist at all, or that it is actually the fault of the customer, or that the problem occurred somewhere else entirely. The tone is so defensive that it is offensive: *Hey there, stupid, I'm doing you a big favor by responding to you at all!*

Surely they don't honestly believe that this approach is going to fool anyone! I know you don't.

If the fault lies in our domain, the best thing we can do is come right out and say so. It doesn't do any harm for us to say we're sorry, as long as we don't grovel about it.

One method used by a highly successful corporation involves the following steps:

1. State the problem, accept the blame matter-of-factly, and apologize briefly. (Do not describe the incoming letter as a "complaint," but simply say something like "In response to your letter . . . . "

2. Spell out exactly what is being done to rectify the mistake. Be specific, paying special attention to such matters as when action will take place. Give specific times and dates.

3. Make sure there are no loose ends. If a wrong shipment is sent, not only send the right one promptly, but be sure to pick up the wrong one at least as promptly! The sight of the wrong merchandise cluttering up the office or the loading dock is a constant reminder of your mistake.

4. Offer some extra benefit, service, price break, or whatever, to help make up for the mistake.

Those four steps are all that need go into your actual dictation, but there is one final step just as important as all these:

5. Follow up with a telephone call, or better still, a personal visit by some high-ranking member of the organization to make sure the customer is satisfied. (As a matter of fact, some companies make it standard practice to call a customer the day after an important shipment is expected to arrive at the customer's dock to check whether it did, in fact arrive . . . and safely. The caller also thanks the customer for buying from the caller's company and asks for future business.)

The success of the corporation that recommends these steps testifies to their effectiveness. I can think of nothing more to add except a fervent "Amen."

Summing Up

Remember to write only when necessary — and that means *dictate* only when necessary. The four main reasons for writing are usually (1) to get information; (2) to give information; (3) to get action; and (4) to affect attitudes. Telephoning will often accomplish the mission effectively — but use the same good techniques for telephoning that you would use for dictating.

- Reserve memos for *internal* communications. Be clear, but don't be stiff or formal. It's okay to use relaxed language, including nicknames and (within the limits of good taste) slang and jargon.

- In "good news" letters, get to the point quickly. Be sincere, gracious, and human. Employ the "you" approach.

- In "bad news" letters, cushion the blow if possible. Prefer a positive to a negative approach — not just in "bad news" letters, but in all your correspondence.

- If you are at fault, say so. Then do your best to make things right.

- Follow up when the situation calls for it — either by telephone, or better still, by a personal visit.

NOTE: Although I had thought it would be obvious that this cartoon is a period piece, reminiscent of the old *College Humor* magazine of the 1930s, my editors have pointed out that all you young readers can't remember as far back as I can. Let me hasten to point out that this cartoon is intended to be satirical, and that *Dictating Effectively,* like *Writing With Precision* before it, has been written in nonsexist style.

I flout those who
flaunt their ignorance.
— Stanley Kunitz, quoted in
Harper Dictionary of Contemporary Usage

11: How to Dictate Without Being Dull

Take a Cliché, Miss Jones

In the days of my youth, the lecherous old businessman and his voluptuous young secretary were standard cartoon characters. The cartoons had regularly recurring themes, employing both visual and written clichés. Even before you looked, you would know that the stereotyped lecherous boss would either be chasing the stereotyped beautiful secretary around the desk, or she would be sitting on his lap, dictation notebook at the ready. The caption would invariable begin with "Take a letter, Miss Jones."

Although the remainder of the caption would be devoted to the punchline, it took little imagination for readers to divine what the rest of the dictation was going to sound like:

```
Dear Mr. Murgatroyd:

Your favor of the 16th inst. has been

received and contents duly noted. We humbly

beg to advise that according to our records,
```

```
your esteemed order was shipped on or about

the 12th inst. Pursuant to the terms of your

request, we are pleased to send you the copy

of Joe Miller's Joke Book to which your order

has entitled you. We appreciate sincerely

your valuable patronage and trust that we may

continue to serve you in the future.

    Thanking you for your many courtesies to us

in the past, we remain, sir

    Your most humble and obedient servant,

    (Signed) Alexander Q. Throttlebottom
```

That kind of archaic language is supposed to have disappeared with the celluloid collar, but an amazing lot of it is still around today — embedded like flies in amber — in the correspondence of supposedly modern companies and organizations.

Today's executive usually picks up a microphone instead of a secretary, at least at dictation time. But chances are, the dictation itself is likely to consist of the same stuffy, pedantic, overblown language of the olden days.

Out of habit, most dictators will somehow manage to put at least one cliché or other wornout phrase in every sentence. I must unwillingly admit that I often do it myself. You'll find plenty of examples in the preceding paragraphs, and I have chosen not to edit any of them out this time — they make such good "bad examples."

"disappeared with the celluloid collar" . . .

"like flies in amber" . . .

Those two unimaginative expressions turned up within a couple of lines when I was dictating this chapter; they came to mind and I said them, I admit it. But I like to think I'm not all that different from other persons dictating everywhere, every day.

The fact is, most of us can't live without clichés — or at least we can't talk without using them. Psychologists tell us that we think in clusters of words, not single words; as it happens, many of those clusters that we have most readily available in our mental storage banks are the clichés I am talking about. When we reach into that mental repository to draw out some quick phrases suitable for the occasion, guess what we are likely to latch onto, almost every time!

If you don't believe all this, try an experiment: dictate a sentence by carefully choosing just one word at a time. Now, pause and ponder. What happened? Chances are, you found the process difficult if not impossible.

Okay, when I tried it, so did I. So do most of us. Which brings up an interesting and practical question. Is it really such a sin for us to use clichés when dictating a first draft? Or should we try to get rid of them — every one of them?

My answer is a qualified "no," but I had better explain, and do it fast. For I am well aware that the purists will tell us to avoid clichés like we would Typhoid Mary. (There's an example of my mind hard at work to come up with a non-cliché version of "like the plague.") They want us to replace each trite expression with a fresh new phrase.

The problem is, of course, that each fresh new phrase takes time. Furthermore, it interrupts the flow of our thought processes. (As Chuck Waterman says, "There's no cliché like an old cliché.")

So here is where I must boldly stick my neck out. I'll even put this controversial suggestion in boldface (that's a pun, son) to prove the courage of my convictions (a cliché?) thus:

During dictation, I firmly believe we should feel free to use as many clichés as we want to, as often as we want to. Thoughts will flow faster and easier, and we are more likely to say what we mean, and say it clearly. (But — please note the disclaimer in the next section!)

After all, how does a cliché get to be a cliché? Why does it stick in the memory of almost everyone, and remain a fixed part of the language for year after year, decade after decade, perhaps even century after century?

I'll answer my own question. A cliché sticks because it is apt. It is a distillation of truth. It says something that most human beings know, feel, and understand, and it says it clearly and well. Furthermore, it says it in the word patterns and clusters that are lurking there in the "word-processing" center of the human mind. Trying desperately to avoid using clichés during dictation — or during speech — is the surest way I know of to turn almost anyone into the strong, silent type. (Another cliché — but it certainly does make me think of Gary Cooper, looking handsome, stern, and a smidgen shy, as he modestly intones his favorite response: "Yup.")

Eat Your Cake and Have It Too

Here, then, is my advice. Use clichés as freely and uninhibitedly as you wish, in either your speech or your dictation. Then, *if you are concerned about your literary style, make a strenuous effort to transform the clichés into fresher language as you go through the editing process.* But if you're not shooting for the Nobel Prize, you won't be committing a crime if a few clichés slip through into your final draft. Frankly, I long ago had to recognize that I had neither the ear nor the talent of a Jim Aswell — if I did you wouldn't find nearly so many clichés in this book. But, within my limitations, I go on and do the best I can. Also, just to muddy up the water (that's a midwestern-ism, but not necessarily a cliché), I'd like to point out that there are degrees and gradations between clichés, idioms, and scholarly allusions. To relieve your conscience, and mine, I'd like to discuss some of these differences.

For example, the heading of this section, "Eat your cake and have it too," might be construed by some as a cliché. Others would say it is instead a well-known proverb, or at least a variation of one, and hence can be excused. After all, proverbs are a writer's (or dictator's) best friend. (That, of course, is a variation of another cliché, or a song title, according to how you look at it, and is hence excusable, or inexcusable, also according to how you look at it.)

Just for fun, (cliché?) let's look at a few of the buzz-words and buzz-phrases that have been the mainstay of business communication in recent years. How many of them do you use? If you strike them from your language, will you be rendered speechless? You may be surprised when you begin to check.

What is the thrust of your report?

Have you considered all the parameters?

Is there a viable alternative?

What was happening at that point in time?

What's the bottom line?

The ball is in your court.

We have reached a watershed point.

This list, of course, only scratches the surface. It comes nowhere near the bottom line. But I hope that reading this chapter will bring you to a watershed point in raising your consciousness. Then, perhaps, in the ongoing future, you may be able to interface a great deal better, try various parameters on for size, and maybe even run a few of them up the flagpole to see who salutes. If you learn to achieve appropriate sequential prioritization, it is not inconceivable that you may be able to maximize the input, minimize the glitches, and eventually kludge together a viable scheme of things.

Indeed, if you would like to continue with an in-depth study to increase your basic confidence factor in mastering the cliché situation on an everyday basis, I suggest you read Edwin Newman's *Strictly Speaking* and *A Civil Tongue*,[9] if you haven't already. I commend them to you —with a warning. By the time you finish reading Mr. Newman's devastating comments on the mistreatment of the English language, you may become so self-conscious you'll be afraid to say a word.

---

9   This book in currently out of print, but you should be able to find it in most libraries.

Jim and Mrs. Malaprop

My old boss, Jim Aswell, used to carpool with a wondrous lady whose way with the English language is unequalled in recent memory (Jim's OR mine.) Every day he would come into the office and relay to us the latest gems:

That junkyard is really a sore eye.

He looked at me with askance.

I don't drink, but I smoke like a fish.

This car can start on a dime.

He waits on her hoof and mouth.

If Jim had saved the collection, he could have written a book. Unfortunately, neither he nor any of the rest of us thought of doing it, so most of those dazzlers, which should have been preserved for posterity, have been lost forever; the few I've salvaged for you are those that happened to lodge in out-of-the-way interstices of my synapses.

The best one of all, I think, I have saved for last. Here is what our favorite malaproprietress said when she heard, back in the 60s, that there was going to be a "Poor People's March on Washington."

It's going to be a mess. I'll just bet you they will all go sleeping around the outlying skirts.

I must admit to a sneaking admiration for anything that has so much rightness, beauty, and wisdom about it. Inspiration was obviously at work. "Sheer elfin genius," as Jim was fond of saying.

The Noble Art of Substitution

Why do I bring up such matters? Because, ludicrous as it may seem, such phrases may open our imaginations to some of the possibilities of the language, and might even suggest a new approach to expressing old ideas. Read anything at all by the wonderful Peter DeVries and you'll see what I mean. (One of my favorites is, "Deep down, he's shallow.")

You might call the technique of substituting new phrases in clichés a matter of "ringing the changes."

Is that expression itself a cliché? No — or at least, not in my opinion. By definition, a cliché is wornout, hackneyed, threadbare. "Ringing the changes" is not used all that much.

I could say that it is not a cliché, but an idiom, or perhaps a somewhat obscure literary (or more accurately, musical) allusion. We'll discuss the differences in a moment.

In my original draft, at one point I dictated a very obvious cliché, the phrase "to your heart's content." Chuck Waterman suggested I change it to read "to your mind's content." That seemed worth doing, and I took his suggestion. It is a hopeful sign when even a mildly new twist can be given to a threadbare expression.

Again, however, I must remind you that the best time to make the change is *after* you have the first draft transcribed on paper. If you strive too desperately to avoid clichés while you are dictating, you may find yourself back in the freeze syndrome we've worked so hard to overcome.

Using Idioms Correctly

Many expressions you might consider clichés may really be idioms instead. What's the difference, and how can you tell?

Sometimes you can't. But if you speak English as your native language, your ear is attuned to most idiomatic expressions so well that you won't even have to think about them. In fact, if you do, you'll discover how funny many of them sound when you try to interpret them literally. Do you really "catch somebody's eye"? How about "falling head over heels"? Don't you really fall "heels over head"? Does the boss really make you "burn the midnight oil"?

My point is simply this: idioms are natural to our speech, and we change them only at our peril. If we try to avoid what we believe to be a cliché by changing the natural idiom peculiar to our strange and wonderful language, we may end up out in *right* field. See what I mean?

Of course, sometimes there can be real art to misusing the idiom. Do you remember how, when the newspapers were talking about the prevalence of immorality at high levels of government, the Reverend Billy Graham made his widely quoted remarks about "shacking down"? I don't know whether to ascribe the usage to innocence or artfulness, but you'll have to admit it's beautiful. In one breath we have the implication that Dr. Graham has theoretical knowledge of the wickedness of the world, but has obtained it at leg's length. That's even longer than "arm's length."

Many years ago, another minister I knew in a small Missouri town perhaps surpassed even Dr. Graham. I can never forget the sermon during which he admonished us wicked teen-age boys to stay out of the local pool hall. "Watch it, boys," he told us, "or one of these days you are all going to end up behind the nine ball."

The moral is, and I think it is very appropriate to have a moral at this point, since I don't want this book to be X-rated:

> **Idioms are valuable and necessary: clichés are "neither of the above." Don't mistake one for the other. Try to freshen up your favorite clichés if you can, and don't use idioms unidiomatically.**

Using Quotations and Literary Allusions

It has been said that quotations and literary allusions are old-fashioned and should have no place in modern writing. Some writers feel that giving any appearance of being the least bit highbrow is a mortal sin. Overdo it, and you may be considered pedantic, or even as someone who espouses the dubious proposition that all expository writing should be propaedeutical. Maybe your readers will even be led to believe that you reside in an ivory tower, where you habitually practice omphaloskepsis. (If I now send you scurrying to an unabridged dictionary, that's exactly what I intended. The late Henry Fairlie's writings often did that to me, and in the process added a few vital words to my vocabulary.)

It would appear that it is okay for us to flout knowledge, but not to flaunt it. I say, "Shucks." (That, dear readers, is a *literary allusion* to E.B. White's marvelous poem about Diego Rivera's murals at Rockefeller Center: "'I paint what I see,' said Rivera." The punchline is worth alluding to here, if my mention should cause you to look it up in the original, which can be found in Seldon Rodman's *Anthology of Modern Poetry.*)

Are literary allusions clichés? I don't think so, but then, like others of my ilk, I consider part of my purpose is to be propaedeutical, and I practice omphaloskepsis in moderation. (Yes, I know that *ilk* is correctly limited to the meaning of *of that same name*; thus, it can only indirectly mean *sort* or *kind*. I consider it pedantic of you to point that out.)

You probably remember the story of the fellow who went to see *Hamlet*, and came out muttering, "I don't see what's so great about that guy Shakespeare—all he does is string clichés together."

You may be damned if you do and damned if you don't—use literary allusions, that is. In my own case, I prefer to be damned if I do, especially when I consider the glorious ambiguity of that statement.

*In composing, as a general rule,
run your pen through every other word
you have written; you have no idea
what vigor it will give to your style.*
— *Sydney Smith*

12: How to Edit Your Own Dictation

Nobody Said It Was Easy

One of the hardest things in the world to do is to edit your own copy. Just because that copy has been transcribed from dictation doesn't make the task any easier.

I suspect that's why so many hotshot dictators choose to request all their letters and memos in "final form." From the looks of things, they must sign this garbage without reading it for even the most obvious faults. They cop out by saying, "I'm much too busy—just don't have time for all this folderol."

Sometimes they add insult to injury by including a notation, "Dictated but not read." My instant response: if the sender hasn't read it, the receiver won't either! (Jim Aswell's answer was: "Received but not read.")

Too bad these arrogant rascals don't take a moment to read their drivel in draft. Even a cursory glance might prevent much mindless nonsense from polluting the U.S. mail.

It's true that a skilled dictator can turn out a reasonably good letter on the first try. The problem is that there are many more people around who consider themselves skilled dictators than there are skilled dictators.

Also, strange as it seems, the truly competent ones who can turn out first-rate copy in one try are most likely to be the ones who still carefully edit that copy before signing.

Is that practice indeed a waste of valuable time?

No way. It probably is the best possible use of that time. There is always a point of diminishing returns, but few of us ever reach it. Once in a great while I've run across perfectionists so meticulous that — deadlines permitting — they keep editing and re-editing for days. When the boss in desperation wrenches the latest revision from reluctant (I almost said "bleeding") fingers, the standard cry is, "Just one more time and it might have been pretty good!"

That's overkill. Obviously it is good sense and good economics to cut off the editing before it becomes its own excuse for being.

Saving Time By Editing Directly On the Tape

Even under tight deadlines, you should still edit your copy. With short letters, you can often edit right on the tape. Many of the new generations of dictation machines permit you to make changes at the exact spot on the tape where they are needed, *without erasing the rest of your recording.* If you get a machine with this and some of the other valuable features now available, you and your transcriber will both save enough time to pay for the extra cost in short order. But, if you are working with a less fancy machine, please don't give up editing. Even though it appears to slow things down a bit, it's still well worth the time and effort.

The Five Steps of Editing

You'll find the whole process much easier if you think of editing as a series of five distinct steps. Here's what you need to know:

STEP ONE: Allow a cooling-off period.

You have doubtless long since discovered that you can't look objectively at *anything* you have written or dictated if you try to do it too soon after completing the creative process. If you can put the draft away for three days or more, you'll be able to look at it with less personal involvement. This enables you to criticize your own work almost as if you were a disinterested third party.

That's marvelous. Unfortunately, in the real world it often simply isn't possible. With tight schedules and short deadlines, this kind of cooling-off period frequently becomes a luxury few can afford. Business success may require that the correspondence go out promptly, and the cooling-off period disappears without a trace.

Roll with the punches, making the most of any time you *do* have. If you have dictated a cassetteful of letters and memos that must go out before nightfall, at least take advantage of the built-in delay while the initial dictation is being transcribed. If your office is anything like mine, there could easily be a period of anywhere from a couple of hours to half a day before your drafts come back. Use that time to work on some completely different project and you'll be better able to take a fresh look when it's time to edit.

The average dictator probably asks for those letters back typed in "final." And I suspect that the standard office practice is for those letters to be signed immediately, with scarcely a second glance.

If that's what has been going on in your office, please stop. Ask for a double-spaced "draft" version first. This needn't be as time-consuming or wasteful as you might suppose. Most modern offices today have word-processing equipment that can store your letters and memos on floppy disks when the first draft is being "keyboarded." This stored information can either be played back verbatim, or edited very quickly, "on screen." Either way, the replay requires only a fraction of the time consumed in the initial tape recording. Because of this time-saving flexibility, you might want to let your secretary transcribe in "final" form, with the mutual understanding that if everything isn't okay, it will be edited and corrected in the "word-processing" playback.

STEP TWO: Read straight through the dictated unit (letter, memo, etc.) without making any editorial marks on it.

Try to get an impression of how the *total* communication flows. Focus your attention on the whole message you seek to convey and the results you want to achieve. If *you* were receiving the letter instead of sending it, would you be persuaded to do what it asks?

> **STEP THREE:** Ask the well-known questions that newspaper reporters are taught to ask: WHO-WHAT-WHERE-WHY-HOW-HOW MANY-HOW MUCH?

These questions may sound so elementary to you that perhaps you see no point in asking them — or answering them. Don't be deceived. They are indeed simple, but they are also essential to a thorough editing process. The first few times you try, you may be shocked to discover a strange phenomenon: facts you have in your head do not always get transferred onto the paper! You'll find out what most self-editors eventually learn — some of the questions you confidently thought were taken care of completely will not withstand close scrutiny. Indeed, they may be just vaguely hinted at, or perhaps even omitted.

Ask the essential questions, one at a time — carefully. Only then can you be positive you've given all the essential answers.

> **STEP FOUR: Apply the Ten Principles of Editing, explained in detail in my book WritingWithPrecision.**

In case you don't have a copy (shame on you), I'll summarize the principles for you here:

1. **Prefer the active voice.**

2. **Don't make nouns out of good, strong "working verbs."**

3. **Be concise. Cut out excess verbiage.**

4. **Be specific. Use concrete terms instead of abstractions or generalizations.**

5. **Keep your modifiers as close as possible to the words they are intended to modify.**

6. **Avoid unnecessary shifts of subject, number, tense, voice, or point of view.** (If you don't understand all these terms, you really had better read *Writing With Precision.*)

7. **Prefer the simple word to the far-fetched, and the right word to the almost right.**

8. **Don't repeat words, phrases, or ideas needlessly. But don't hesitate to repeat when the repetition will increase clarity.**

9. **Make sentence elements that are parallel in thought parallel in form.**

10. **Arrange your material logically.**

While you're beginning, try applying these principles one at a time. Before long, you'll be able to handle many, or even all of them, at the same time.

| **STEP FIVE: Read the draft aloud.** |

By so doing, you may detect faulty sentences, poor word choices, or bad connotations that you might otherwise overlook. During my years as a professional speechwriter, I learned that the ear is an extremely acute detection device.

Let's Have a 'For Instance'

The manuscript of this book went through four separate drafts and self-editings in the original edition. This 1990 updating adds a couple more. On top of that, a number of my friends and associates in the writing and editing business have given it their best editorial shots. In spite of all this painstaking care, however, all of us who deal regularly with publishing know from bitter experience that embarrassing errors will slip into print.

Murphy's Law!

You might find it instructive to track a few lines of manuscript through a copy of editing stages. The next page shows reproductions of actual versions of the typed manuscript of this book. The penciled-in editings show changes as the work progressed.

(Version One)

ADD PRODUCTIVE HOURS TO YOUR DAY
              DO   for
        [Have] you ever wished there were] more hours in the day? Wondered] how you
     can finish   staying
[were going to get] that report [finished] before deadline without [having to]

[stay] up all night? Looked] at that big stack of letters waiting in your
                                       'll
in-basket and wondered] how you['d] ever get them all answered?
                                           has plenty of members.
      [So, if you have--]welcome to the club. It [is a very large one indeed.]
                                         it   years,
[And, I might add, one that] I have belonged to,^for [longer than most of you]
           and   The
[have lived.] ʅ just resigned [from it] this year. [Its] membership is made up
         ly   people   can't--or won't--
[in] large,[measure] of [those of us] who [persist in remaining in the Stone Age;]

[those who refuse to] learn to dictate.

(Version Two)

ADD PRODUCTIVE HOURS TO YOUR DAY
            often yearn
      Do you [ever wish] for more hours in the day? Wonder how [you can] finish
                                         working   Dreadfacing
that report before deadline without [staying up] all night? [Look at that big]
 [that mountain)   despairof ever
[stack] of letters waiting in your in-basket, and [wonder how you'll ever get]
         ^ cutting it down to a molehill?
[them all answered?]
                    Time Trap   Its millions of members
      Welcome to the/club--[it has plenty of members.] I belonged to it for years,]
                                          are mostly
[and just resigned this year. The membership is made up largely of] people who

can't--or won't--learn to dictate.

(Version Three)

TIMELINESS IS NEXT TO GODLINESS

      Do you often yearn for more hours in the day? Wonder how to finish that

report before deadline without working all night? Dread facing that mountain

of letters overflowing your in-basket, and despair of ever cutting it down to

a molehill?

      Welcome to the Time Trap Club. Its millions of members are mostly people

who can't or won't learn to dictate. I belonged for years. Now I've resigned;

please join me as a Member Emeritus, mastering time instead of letting it

master us.

Taking a hard look at this final version, you may get the feeling that I should have run it through the wringer at least one more time. Oh well, nobody's "prefect."

Summing Up

Good dictating is good editing. If you want to dictate like a professional, learn to edit like a professional — thoroughly, accurately, and speedily.

Edit your copy in stages:

---

1. Allow a cooling-off period.
2. Read straight through to get an impression of the **total** communication.
3. Ask the questions WHO-WHAT-WHEN-WHERE-WHY-HOW-HOW MANY-HOW MUCH?
4. Apply the Ten Principles of Editing; at first, apply the principles one at a time — then, as your skill increases, you can do several at once.
5. Read the draft aloud to detect mistakes you might otherwise miss.

It usually takes me more than three weeks
to prepare a good impromptu speech.
— Samuel Clemens ("Mark Twain")

13: How to Dictate Speeches

Speaking Your Mind

Why do some speeches sound so good? And others so bad?

The way I see it, the bad ones sound bad because they don't sound like *speech*.

What they *do* sound like is writing, and usually not very good writing — stiff, stilted, pedantic, and frequently awkward. Because good writing usually does sound something like speech.

When I was a professional speechwriter, I didn't know how to dictate. Had I but known! For 13 years I was trying to write speeches that sounded like speech, and I was doing it the hard way. The way to make a speech sound like speech is to dictate. By going that route, the speechwriter saves many intermediate steps, and turns out higher quality work in a fraction of the time. (Although I am not exactly humble about the quality or quantity of the speeches I did produce — after all, I'm a Leo.)

Anyway, before writing this chapter, I had not actually dictated a speech. I'd been getting quite a bit of practice by dictating the earlier parts of this book, but I decided that to avoid being fraudulent, I had better dictate a speech and try out my techniques.

Because all my professional speechwriting experience at NASA involved tight deadlines, I decided I had better recreate the conditions by painting myself into a corner. A phony deadline wouldn't do. So I called up the educational vice president of Fairfax Toastmasters Club No. 1899, and volunteered to give a 10-minute educational speech on "How to Dictate a Speech." The deadline was short, there was no escape, and I was thus able to put myself into the frame of mind that is most natural to me when doing a speechwriting assignment.

The fun part was that at least I was writing a speech I could deliver myself. I've had all I want of putting words in other people's mouths.

Brainstorming On Tape

With an appearance scheduled, a deadline set, and my mind in its proper state of controlled crisis, I was ready to begin. Because my chosen subject was a how-to-do-it on dictating speeches, I had the advantage of being able to pull things together in a much more practical way than if I had just sat myself down to dictate another chapter.

I began to feel a sense of exhilaration that isn't exactly common among professional speechwriters. Here was my chance to draw on all my experience, and come up with an approach to dictating speeches that (to my knowledge) had never been described in a book before. So, all fired up, I dug out a batch of 5x8 cards and began the old brainstorming game. Okay, I said to myself, what are the basics of dictating a good speech? What techniques of speechwriting can I easily carry over? What things must I do differently?

Revelation! For the first time in my speechwriting career, I suddenly discovered that I wasn't really quite ready for the cards yet. I began to speak my brainstorming ideas straight onto the cassette.

(The following material is a transcription, in raw, completely unedited form, of the cassette I used to dictate the basic material for this chapter. I recognize all too well that the thoughts are often rambling and disjointed, but that's the only honest way I can show you what happened.)

"Okay, what are the basics of dictating a good speech? Very similar to the basics of other dictation in many ways — let's look at both the similarities and the differences. Obviously, the first step is to pick your theme and narrow it down. I've done that — HOW TO DICTATE A SPEECH is a good descriptive title that tells a story, and a good title is an important step, although not always the first one. (I often used to save it until last, actually.)

Next, you must support that theme. A good "standard" speech of about ten minutes can make three major points in support. Somewhere along the way I am going to have to decide on what those major points will be.

But — before you present your supporting arguments, you have to have a grabber. I think I will talk about two different kinds of speeches — those used in Toastmasters, and those that you'd use on the lecture circuit or before a "real world" audience.

I believe in Toastmasters, and have learned a lot from belonging. I joined late in life, and writing and delivering speeches for myself has been an educational and rewarding experience.

But one thing I must explain to the Toastmasters audience is that the seven minutes (with a "grace period" of another 30 seconds) maximum for a usual Toastmasters speech is not even a beginning in a speech for the real world. Seven minutes is hardly enough to wind yourself up and get off the ground.

So, in TM, everything must be very intensive. All the Toastmasters I know try to have really dramatic grabbers — often red-hot controversial statements, or provocative questions, or whatever. And they make sure to shoot for audience attention with that grabber by putting it in the very first sentence. Also, they deliver it as dramatically as possible.

In such a tightly structured format, you can't afford to waste a word. You have to make sure you get all your points across and finish before that seven-minute deadline disqualifies you.

In the real world, suppose you are making a speech after one of those well-known rubber-chicken banquets. It's a different situation entirely. The audience is probably starting to get sleepy. Most of them have had a few drinks and a big meal. They are probably getting a bit "antsy" about going to the bathroom.

Also, they are going to be talking to their table mates, and making plenty of noise and commotion.

So, if you plan to start with a TM type of blockbuster in your first sentence, you have to be out of your mind. What a professional speaker would do is allow anywhere from 20 to 40 seconds or so for the audience to start shaping up and giving their undivided attention. This is what Jim Aswell called the "throwaway."

Ladies and Gentlemen . . . Thank you for inviting me here this evening . . . It's a great pleasure to be here with such an august group . . . your president, Mr. Himmelfarb, is one of nature's noblemen . . . blah, blah, blah.

In other words, the speaker is not saying anything at this point — just expressing thanks and appreciation. That's important. After all, the organization is picking up your tab, and — I hope — paying you a handsome honorarium as well. But you don't have to leap instantly into the fray — or the frying pan. (Sorry, tape, couldn't resist that!)

The throwaway lead gives a chance for the conversations to wind down, the audience to scoot their chairs into a new position, shuffle their feet, and prepare to give some modicum of attention. THEN — you are ready for the grabber. Say it very distinctly and not too fast. Probably you should pause for a few seconds before you say it — make it sound momentous.

Planning and Organizing

That's enough of the raw dictation. I wanted to give a sense and flavor of what was happening, and I must admit I surprised myself. I had intended just to speak some points onto the tape, and I found that my mind was not working that way—so, since the words were flowing freely, I chose not to interrupt the flow. That's important—even if the ideas you are dictating are not what you expected them to be, don't interrupt the flow. Something good might come out of it, and if not, you can always erase the tape and try again.

When the spontaneity began to fade, I felt it was time to return to my original purpose. In a way I had been warming myself up for the main event, and giving my mind a chance to relax and free-wheel a bit before settling down to business. I knew I had a subject that promised to be interesting to my audience, and I had enough of a store of knowledge, anecdotes, true-life experiences (many of them fiascoes), to put together a dozen speeches on the subject. I had to pick and choose. So now I began to dictate in terms of separate ideas or steps.

STEP ONE is, of course, choosing a subject and narrowing it to the point that it can be discussed within the time allotted. I had already done that.

STEP TWO is to pick some key points—preferably the magic three—to support the topic.

STEP THREE is to think of some anecdotes or illustrations, preferably one for each point.

STEP FOUR is to think of a provocative grabber. While thinking of a short, punchy lead, you may come up with some ideas for titles at the same time. (As I have said, I chose my title first in this instance, but usually I choose it last.)

STEP FIVE is to plan an effective close that sums up your whole message—memorably. "Tell 'em you told 'em." No speechwriter should ever be allowed to forget the trite and homely truism of the old Baptist minister who said, "Tell 'em you're going to tell 'em, tell 'em, and tell 'em you told 'em." Like many other truisms, it happens to be true.

At this point it was time to put some of these ideas down on my cards. As always I was not concerned about orderly arrangement or trying to put first things first. Just get the ideas down fast, some kind of a way.

On one card I wrote "Dictating machine – good attention grabber – use for prop."

On another I wrote, "Speech within a speech?"

On still another, "Tape part of speech and play back as dictation example." (A brilliant idea that sadly went wrong. I'll tell you about how Murphy's Law struck again, but not until later in the chapter.)

Speech Blocks – Keeping Your Options Open

On another card I wrote, "Explain speech blocks."

Then I stopped writing on my cards, because I suddenly wanted to dictate some more. I'm hyped on the idea of "speech blocks," which is what we called them at NASA. I'm sure Jim Aswell and I didn't invent them, and perhaps professional speechwriters everywhere use them. I frankly don't know. What I do know is how well the system worked for us. So let me replay for you here a bit more of my raw dictation:

At NASA we almost always wrote in what we called speech blocks, which usually ranged from one to three double-spaced pages per block, or roughly anywhere from 300 to 900 words.

I'd better explain some fundamentals here. The average speaker talks at a rate of about 140 words a minute, give or take. Some are much faster, some a bit slower. But if you figure on 140, you won't go too far wrong during the drafting stages.

A page of typed manuscript, double-spaced, will contain somewhere between 250 and 325 words, again speaking very roughly. So it follows that each page of manuscript will take the speaker about two minutes to deliver. (In practice, especially if the speaker is READING the manuscript, it may go faster – perhaps a good deal faster. But before a live audience, most speakers slow down. Responding to feedback from the audience, the speaker will undoubtedly pause more than during the practice session.)

I know from my own experience that if something I say gets a laugh, even a small one, my tendency is to want to milk it for all it is worth. Maybe other speakers have more character than I do (I fervently hope so), but few can resist hamming things up a bit for an appreciative audience.

Anyway, back to speech blocks. The trick is to pick one of your support points, introduce it and explain it as briefly as possible. (Don't be TOO brief—you have to make sure the audience fully understands what you are driving at.) Then you illustrate. Use picture words. Give concrete examples. Paint a vivid word picture, so clearly that members of the audience can almost SEE what it is you are talking about. Make sure the whole speech block is a total and coherent entity, and try to make it stand on its own feet, without regard to anything else that is going into the speech.

Do more speech blocks, always using the same technique. This keeps your options open, because you can later push the blocks around and try them at different places in the speech until you determine the arrangement that is most effective. Also, with a number of such speech blocks tucked away in your file cabinet, you can break them out and put them together in the nearest thing possible to an instant speech, the next time the word comes down that you must turn out a complete speech ready for delivery at three o'clock this afternoon. (And don't think that doesn't happen all too often. I'm reminded of how glad I am to be out of the professional speechwriting business.)

Polishing the Tape

When I finished this bit of spontaneous dictation, I went back to the cards once more, and began to fill in and augment. I made a card for the grabber, writing down "This little machine can change your life." I was thinking in terms of using a cassette recorder as a visual aid; the idea would be to hold it up briefly before the audience, then put it down on the lectern and turn it on to record the speech itself. At the end, I intended to play back a small portion of the tape as a demonstration, then stop it and "tell 'em I told 'em."

The speech began to take shape before my eyes. I would make it a case history of how I had dictated the speech itself. Remember that I had one card saying "Speech within a speech"? The gimmick on that was to weave in and out of the case history, demonstrating what happened at each point, and still delivering a speech that lived up to the rules and followed the steps. Neat, what?

Ordinarily, B.D. (that stands for "before dictation," remember?), at this point I would have hied myself to my word processor and started typing out a draft of this speech. This time I didn't. I started dictating again, using my cards as guides, and dictated a speech block for each card, just freewheeling and rambling along.

Then I played it back, hoping for a miracle. It didn't happen. The speech was pretty bad, and as we say in the trade, the plumbing showed. The seams were obvious, the transitions more so. I hadn't made proper use of what is sometimes called the "thread." That's what holds the total structure together into a coherent piece.

Whatever it lacked, one thing was sure. It sounded like *me* talking, with the natural rhythms of my own speech. And the matter of rhythms reminded me of some extremely important tips Jim Jeffries gave me on this subject when he reviewed my manuscript. They are so important I must pass them on to you.

For Professional Ghostwriters Only

Said Jim: "The beauty of dictating a speech for yourself is that it *does* sound right for you—the natural flow, the word choices, the speech rhythms, do not have the phony, stiff-collar sound that you get in a typewritten first draft. Great! But if you are writing a speech for someone else, look out—for the words you dictate so naturally for yourself won't be that natural for somebody else."

"Jim," I said, "that sounds logical to me, but the truth is, I've never actually *dictated* a speech for anyone else. Can you fill me in a bit more?"

"Glad to," he said. "I've dictated dozens of them. Let me tell you what I learned the hard way.

"The key is to use your recorder when you interview your principal. You might want to back up the tape with a few notes, but that's up to you. What I always make sure to do is to get enough samples of my principal's manner of speaking during the interview to capture the flavor of the style. During playback, I listen for favorite words and phases. Just as important, I determine the average number of words between breaths—what I call the 'natural rhythm' of the speaker.

"Not only do I play the tape a number of times to get an aural impression of the speaker, but I also write down some of the words and phrases as reminders. Then, when I am ready to start dictating, I use these as aids to help me think and speak in a way that will be comfortable for my principal."

"The thing is," Jim concluded, "an experienced ghostwriter is used to thinking within these confines when handwriting or typing a speech, but it takes a much more conscious effort to do it with a dictating machine."

Okay, folks, you can thank Jim Jeffries for these valuable tips. My excuse for not bringing them up myself is the same one Samuel Johnson once used when a lady asked him why he had misdefined a word in his dictionary. "Ignorance, madam—sheer ignorance!"

Revising On the Dictating Machine

Back to my narrative. As I was saying, I didn't like my first dictated speech efforts, but I didn't erase them. I kept them on tape, and started recording again, dictating additional versions right behind the first attempts. Remember, except for the cards, I still had nothing on paper. B.D., I would have felt panic-stricken or worse. Not now. There was still plenty of tape left; I told myself it was just for fun, relaxing my mind much the way I had done earlier in trying to conquer my dictaphobia. And this time, the speech really began to track. The pieces started falling into place and I detected the first small rosy glow of accomplishment that, in the writing business, is sometimes more important than the pay.

I decided to quit while I was ahead. I dropped the whole bit and went on to something else. That night, I followed my routine of many years, and looked over all my cards and notes again just before going to sleep. And next morning I took a couple more shots at the cassette, still without erasing any of the earlier versions. That doesn't mean that I went back and played all the versions over again each time. Usually I would rewind the cassette just to "zero setting" (set the counter at zero again each time a new version begins) to save time. I figured that the various versions might make a good case history of the speech – a "laboratory curiosity," if nothing else.

Along the way, I began to discover the fringe benefits. Playing a version and trying a new one was a great exercise for improving the timing and inflection. I began to get more comfortable with the material, and the delivery flowed better. This was something I hadn't even thought about. And still I didn't have a written draft. Revolution in the making.

Maybe the draft was just a crutch, I decided. What would happen if? Wow. It was almost too frightening. Even when I was entering speech contests back in the 70s, I had always outlined all my key points fully on note cards. And I had also carefully written out every word, edited and re-edited, as meticulously as I knew how. The difference might be too much for me. So the next time I played the tape back, I pulled out – and transcribed – the material that seemed particularly apt or useful. I didn't try to get every word; I just put the "good stuff" down in my own form of shorthand.

Never Forget Murphy

The time for the speech was drawing near. My confidence was growing. The speech was improving. I began to know the material by heart, and a misguided attack of bravery set in. I decided to deliver the speech without a script. In fact, I went a step farther than that – I decided to deliver it without notes. With my sieve-like memory and snapping synapses, that was a bold decision indeed.

Meeting night came. I awaited my turn, trusty cassette recorder at the ready (or so I thought.) My speech topic was announced, I was introduced, and I stepped confidently to the lectern. After an appropriate pause, I held up the recorder and – maintaining full eye contact with my audience (no notes, remember) – delivered the grabber: *This little machine can change your life.*

I paused, put the machine down on the lectern, pressed the "record" button, and – nothing happened. That was when the horrible truth struck me. Or more accurately, Murphy's Law struck me. *If anything can possibly go wrong, it will.* I had picked up a fresh cassette just before leaving home, but hadn't inserted it in the machine. I knew exactly where it was — nestling snugly on the front seat of my old VW. My beautiful plan of attack was falling apart before my eyes.

I gathered up my courage and went on. My evaluators told me afterward that I had kept my cool — nobody detected that my best-laid plan had "gang agley." And, if I do say so, the interlocking idea of explaining how to use dictation techniques and delivering the instructions in a well-constructed speech was going well. Until — with no notes, and no tape to play back during the final minutes of the speech to illustrate my points before coming in with the clincher, I suddenly lost the whole trend of my thought.

The last four minutes of the speech were off the top of my shiny head, and to this day I don't have the faintest idea what I said, or if any of it made sense. What could have been one of my better speeches went into a tailspin and never pulled out. What's worse, I didn't have the tape when the speech was over, to use as an example for this chapter. (**NOTE:** *Happily, the Toastmasters who critiqued the speech apparently liked it better than I did. There were very few negative comments. I suppose that proves you can fool some of the people some of the time. Or maybe that they are just basically kind-hearted.*)

But the experience, though chastening, was not a total loss. I laboriously went through the earlier stages and reconstructed everything as best I could: I was able to salvage considerable useful material, enough to put the chapter together.

Summing Up (Lessons Learned)

1. Think out loud on the tape. You might be surprised at some of the great ideas that turn up. Try to settle on main points to be made, with an anecdote to illustrate each one.

2. Think of a good title and a grabber.

3. Play back each new recorded version; study what you've taped, and try again. Each new attempt will build naturally on what has gone before.

4. When you find out how well dictating works in putting a speech together, **don't get overconfident. Take the same pains and the same precautions you would use if you were writing out the script in advance.**

5. Don't do what I did — do what I SAY. **Transcribe the final version and put down the major points on cards.** (If you're used to using notes, don't try to wing it!)

6. Practice. (And tape what you practice. You'll learn a lot about how to improve your phrasing and delivery.)

Okay, folks, you've been cautioned — now it's up to you. You can be sure I'll know better next time, and I hope you will, too.

Production is not the application
of tools to materials,
but logic to work.
— Peter Drucker

14: How to Dictate Reports

What's the Problem?

Many reports should never see the light of day. My first advice to anyone assigned the project of writing a report is to get out of the task if possible. That comment is not entirely facetious. What I mean is that the report writer should begin by researching published literature to find out what is already in print on the subject.

The wheel is being re-invented almost every day. At NASA, for example, they still tell about a large aerospace company working on Project Mercury—the company spent about $2 million and a year of research time on a feasibility study. When the report was finally written and published, THEN came the bad news—a rival firm had performed a similar study, come up with the same findings, and *their* published report could have been purchased for about fifteen dollars. This sounds much too true to be apocryphal.

So before you begin to think about dictating *anything*, get yourself to the library, enlist the aid of the librarian, and find out who has published what. Even if this doesn't save you from having to write your own report, knowing what is already in print will enable you to do your job a whole lot better.

Most reports, one way or another, start with a problem. In writing the report, your job is to come up with a solution or solutions. What better way to do that than to find out the solutions recommended by those who have preceded you? Take notes — I don't know how I'd ever get anything done without notecards — but add to them with your handy cassette recorder. Not only will you save time, but chances are you'll be much more complete in your note-taking, because the tape makes it so much easier to do.

Determining Your Audience (see also Chapter Seven)

Too many times during my years in this business, I have picked up reports that were written as if the author had never bothered to decide what audience the report was supposed to be aiming at. One minute the language would be technical enough to baffle anyone but a graduate engineer. The next, there would be some Dick-and-Jane drivel guaranteed to offend any reader over the age of seven. Even if the reports were put together by a committee (and far too many are), the one person in charge of the overall project should make it a point to check for consistency and pull the viewpoint and the intended audience into the same ballpark.

This seems too obvious to say it again, but say it I must. To an even greater extent than is the case with letters and memos, the make-up of your audience must determine the way you must craft your report. Will most of the readers be highly trained experts? Rank beginners? Technically oriented? Or worst of all, a mixture of individuals with totally different backgrounds, training, and even vocabularies?

Whatever the audience, your report must communicate. It must be as clear and straightforward as you know how to make it, without either writing over the heads of the nontechnical persons or writing down to the technical experts.

Not only must you know who will be in your audience, but you must also know what they will be using your report for. Why has the report been requested? For example, should you put in a section that can be used directly as a manual for operations or maintenance people? Should you put in experimental procedures? Should you make the report a complete package in itself, capable of "standing on its own feet," or should you tie it in with some other work(s), perhaps as one report in a series?

As you consider all these things, the old subconscious mind once again will spring to your rescue. Mulling these thoughts over is just one more part of the process of getting everything sorted out, so that when you actually begin to dictate a logical arrangement of your thoughts will come much more easily.

Visualizing the Total Report

- **Cover** — including the title of the report, the name(s) of the author(s), the name of the organization producing the report, and other information as appropriate.

- **Title page** — which usually includes (as does the cover), the title of the report, the name(s) of the author(s), plus the date, the department, and sometimes an identifying control number. (NOTE: In picking your title, try to choose one that is brief but still reasonably definitive. Many technical reports have titles a mile long; they cross over the line from being complete to being ridiculous. I suspect nothing I say here will change things much, but I'd like to put in a plea for holding down the length of the title as much as possible without misleading or confusing the reader.)

- **Letter of transmittal** — Not all reports have these, but most do. Often the transmittal letter is in boilerplate language, but sometimes it must be tailored for the particular situation.

- **Summary or Abstract** — This is a tightly boiled-down version of the overall report, in the fewest words needed to do the job. Sometimes a single sentence will suffice. It tells in a nutshell what was accomplished by the work described in the report, answering the question, "What was done about the subject of this report?"
    You should resist any temptation to make the summary an introduction. (Many writers do not write the summary until the very last thing; a few persons I know, however, take a crack at this early in the game because they say it helps clarify their thinking; if you decide to go about it this way, be prepared to rewrite or edit substantially after finishing the report proper.)

- **Table of Contents** — This should eventually contain all headings and subheadings, spaced to show their relative importance and the way they relate to one another. (At this point, of course, you are not going to fill it in with any detail. Right now you are just giving yourself a chance to put your subconscious to work in visualizing the project as a whole. Eventually the table of contents will be made up of the outline from which you prepare the report itself, and I've already told you the easy way of doing that.

- **List of Figures and Tables** — This is what you get when you eventually assemble your graphic and tabular material and arrange it in the order you want to have it in your report. Again, this will take better shape as your work progresses, but it will help save much writing by reminding you to make your presentation as graphic as possible. Those of us who are word-oriented need to be reminded of how much we can help our readers to think in terms of illustrations as well.

- **Introduction** — This is the part that tells the reader what the problem is, and why it is important enough to bother about. What were the objectives of the work that has been done? How does this work fit in with what has gone before? What is the scope of the job? Where did it start and where did it stop?

- **The Discussion** (sometimes called the **Body of the Report**) — Here is where you give chapter and verse of all the good stuff you have figured out. Although you have mentioned the objectives of your work in a previous section or sections, you may still want to mention them again here, possibly in expanded form. If you restate each objective as you introduce the related topic(s), you will help the reader to follow your reasoning.

- **The Conclusion** — In this part you sum up, as briefly and succinctly as you can, the results of all your study. Here you should bear in mind the reader who must skim a hundred reports a day. Even though you are trying to make things short and sweet, you need to include sufficient detail to give readers a good idea of what the report is all about without their having to read it from start to finish.

Here are some questions the **Conclusion** should answer: "What is the most important thing this study has shown, and what does it mean? What is the next most important thing . . . and the next?"

- **Appendix** — Many report writers don't properly understand or use the Appendix. It can be a life-saver. Here is where you can put highly detailed information, statistics, special background information, and the like. Many readers may totally ignore this section, but specialists will love it. By separating this material, which is likely to bore most readers, from the body of your report, you will speed things up and make the report proper more pleasant for the majority of readers.

- **Bibliography** — This is where you list all your sources. Show author(s), title, publisher, place of publication, and date of publication. Make it easy for readers to find the same sources you used. However, one word of warning is in order here. Don't frustrate readers by listing "classified" sources, out-of-print items or items that are difficult or impossible to obtain; if you must mention such documents, make sure to indicate the status so as not to send anyone on a wild goose chase.

Dictation Time

Now that you have done all your homework and your visualizing, you are ready to start applying the same kind of dictation techniques that we have been discussing all through this book. I am still hooked on the index card system to the extent that I suggest making out such cards for all major subject heads; then put any notations on them that will guide your thoughts as you begin to dictate.

With the appropriate card(s) before you, start right in. Go at the task in a free-wheeling way, without slowing down any more than you can help. Get that first version down on the tape as quickly and fully as possible, with no regard for style or word choice. Get the facts, and get them complete. Do NOT do what some dictators do, and read off your reference material from notecards onto tape. It will be easier for the transcriber to work directly from the cards themselves. Just indicate on your tape where the cards fit in, and use a uniform numbering system to do it.

Don't be afraid of occasional informality, no matter how serious the subject of your report. It will make the dictation more interesting and more fun for you, and you can decide later whether to leave something in or take it out. My theory is that if the subject matter is on the dull side, at least the language that describes it can liven it up a bit now and then.

When your dictation has been transcribed, read it over to make sure you haven't left out anything important. Ask the same old questions: WHO-WHAT-WHERE-WHEN-WHY-HOW-HOW MUCH? Are you satisfied that you have put in everything you need? Chances are, you will find some gaps. Now is the time to fill them in.

Clean-Up Time

First draft complete? Are you sure? Okay, now clean up the mess. Don't spare the blue pencil—give your brainchild hell, preferably after a long enough cooling-off period to give you a bit of perspective. And then comes the time to enlist the aid of your peers. I have the good fortune to know a number of topflight editors, and I cajole as many of them as I can into looking over my material. Lord knows it is a painful process. Chuck Waterman sends my drafts back looking like they've been tracked up by a chicken with red ink on its feet; I think he likes to use red ink instead of a blue pencil because he wants to make sure he has my full attention. If that's his aim, he has succeeded—sometimes I feel as if the pages are splattered with my heart's blood.

Even if you decide not to buy every word of every suggested change—and being hardheaded, I sometimes persist in doing things my own way, right or wrong—the suggestions of persons whose opinions you respect are bound to make you take a harder look and help you turn out a better end product.

And now comes the happy ending. Simply finishing the final draft of a report is enough to lift a great weight off your mind or your back or wherever you've been carrying it. Perhaps even better is the euphoria that comes when you suddenly comprehend the real joy of *no more rewriting— no more editing!*

Savor it. To my way of thinking, those two short statements in italics are some of the most beautiful words in the English language.

Unprovided with original learning,
unformed in the habits of thinking,
unskilled in the arts of composition,
I resolved to write a book.
— Edward Gibbon (1737-1794)

15: How to Dictate Books

Case History of a Laboratory Experiment

The best way I know of telling you how to dictate a book is to give you a case history of this one. As I have told you too many times already, the entire first draft of this book was dictated between Thanksgiving and Christmas 1979. In a very real sense it was a laboratory experiment; in the dictation I tested many techniques the book describes. To learn more about the total process from both sides of the desk, I even transcribed, both by handwriting and by typing, several chapters of my own dictation.

The transcribed first draft was edited, re-edited, and edited again, putting to a practical test the methods described in Chapter Eleven. Thus, using an approach that was debugged several times along the way, I've put into this book everything that works, and have tossed out many techniques that seemed functional at the time but couldn't stand the test of actual practice.

I'll stick to a chronological approach whenever I can, partly because that is often the best and simplest system for both writer (read *dictator* in this case) and reader. If I leave the chronology occasionally, it will be to give you a discussion of something I consider important that doesn't want to fit into the chronology. Sometimes that happens. When it does, I will try to keep things on track by typographic devices (different type face, for example) or other dodges that professional writers use in such circumstances.

Doing My Homework

I started the book by doing what anyone should always do when undertaking a new project. I began investigating to find out what was already in print on the subject that might help. So I buzzed merrily over to the Fairfax County Central Library and checked the catalog.

I made an extremely interesting discovery.

At that time (1979), the Fairfax County Library system contained 1,357,788 books, but it did not have a single book on the art of dictation — not one. I couldn't believe it, so I decided to check some more. I took the Metro down to Washington's fine Martin Luther King Library and checked the catalog there. Sure enough, no book on dictation. Lots of books on how to *transcribe* the dictation. Absolutely none on *how to dictate.*

Chuck Waterman couldn't believe it either. At the time, he was working on an article about the Library of Congress — the greatest library in the world. He volunteered to research the subject during his next visit. Chuck's reputation for accuracy and thoroughness is well known; I was confident that if *anything* on the subject existed in print, Chuck would track it down.

It didn't take him long. Next day he called from the LC to say he had found a few items listed that appeared to have something to do with the art of dictating. Never satisfied with half-measures, he offered to check them out for me, either literally or figuratively. He went on to say, however, that the latest copyright date shown on any of the items was 1957.

SPECIAL NOTE: When Chuck and I did our research in 1979, this statement was true. As we went to press in July 1980, it no longer was: I held this manuscript too long in my bleeding fingers. Early in 1980, Auren Uris, well-known writer on business subjects, beat me to the punch. His book, *Mastering the Art of Dictation*, contains some excellent material. I recommend it to you. But please make sure you read it in addition to my book, not instead of. I try hard to be fair, but not that fair!

I breathed a sigh of relief and asked him not to bother. Technology had moved on by light years in the 60s and 70s (and even more in the 80s). By today's standards, the state of the art of dictation back in 1957 was still in the equivalent of the Dark Ages.

I began to get excited. I don't believe this, I said to myself. (I talk to myself more and more these days.) *Hundreds of thousands of executives, managers, salespersons, and professionals dictating every day, yet no one has bothered to publish a book commercially on how to do it properly.*

Continuing this fascinating interior monologue, I remarked inelegantly, in terms not at all resembling my customary refined diction. *Hot dog! This project is going to move onto the front burner. I've got a chance to break new ground – use myself as a guinea pig, and then take what I learn and help other folks profit from my experience.*

Consulting the Experts

There is an old saying among professional writers; "If you talk too much about a book before you write it, you'll never get around to writing it."

That may be so if you are going to *write* it, but if you are going to *dictate* it, that's a whole new ball game. Actually, talking with others about your project is probably good practice for your later dictation. It certainly was in my case.

I began going around talking to everyone I knew who had any experience dictating. What I found out was extremely helpful, even though I ended up having to learn many things the hard way.

I started with my associates, Lou Hampton and Chuck Waterman. Both were experienced dictators. They were able to teach me right away about some of the mechanical details of effective dictation; unfortunately, not all of these lessons soaked in until I began trying to put them into actual 'practice. Thorndike was right when he said we learn by doing.

Card Systems, Brainstorming, and Variations on an Old Theme

As you know by now, index cards have always been the heart of my system for outlining any long piece of work. I've used the system too long to abandon it now, but I did work in many variations that would never have occurred to me B.D. (before dictation). After each interview or conversation, I played back the cassette and pulled the important ideas off onto cards—one idea per card, as always. In addition, from long habit I made many cards directly without even bothering to dictate them first. I just did what came naturally, and ended with the best of both worlds.

You can get a very good idea of what went onto the cards by looking at the index of this book; I had at least one card for just about every item you find listed as a heading or subheading. At first, of course, they were in no special order; but I'm getting ahead of myself. The easiest way to explain right here is to quote the procedures set forth in my earlier book, *Writing With Precision*, and augment them as appropriate:

- **Get a batch of notecards.** (Preferably 5x8, or 3x5s in continuous format.)

- **Brainstorm.** Throw your imagination into high gear, and start putting down ideas about your project. If you can persuade fellow workers or colleagues who are familiar with your project to help you—and this is what the term "brainstorming" really means, the way it is done in advertising agencies—by all means do so. Creativity is compounded; one idea sparks another. (Remember, no one is allowed to criticize anyone else's idea, no matter how far out it may seem at the time.)

If you end up like the little red hen, with no help, apply the brainstorming process on yourself. Turn your subconscious mind loose. You don't have to know or care where a particular idea is going to fit. All you need do is write it down. Maybe it will eventually land in the first section, or the middle, or the last. You couldn't (or needn't) care less at this point. (NOTE: Apply the process at your most creative time of day—for most of us that would be fairly early in the morning, but not if you are a night person.)

- **Put each idea down on a separate card.** (Just a few words will be sufficient—write only enough to remind you of the idea later.)

- **Use a fresh card for the next idea.** As soon as you complete a card, put it aside. The beauty of this approach is that it frees you from the whole routine of having to figure out in advance what is important. You aren't concerned with what is going to be subordinated to what. It is really a joyful experience to be so free and easy, and to know that you are not locking yourself in.

- **Work on a different project for the rest of the day.** This is important — it relaxes your mind so that when you tackle the job again, you'll be fresh and ready for it.

- **Take the cards home with you; read through them just before you go to sleep.** That way, your subconscious mind will do much of the hard work for you. Try it. It works.

- **Next morning, spread out the cards where you can see them.** As you try arranging the cards in various sequences, you can begin shaping them up into an increasingly logical order. As you proceed, you may move cards forward or back in the sequence as ideas begin to gel. Put closely related cards in the same row or stack.

- **When you finally get the cards into an order you like, use them to make a formal outline.** You're safe in doing this, **because** your options are still open. The outline isn't engraved on stone, so if things don't work out quite right, you can always shuffle the deck and try again. (Incidentally, when I was writing speeches at NASA, I never threw any of those cards away. Sometimes by a bit of thoughtful shuffling, I could come up with several different speeches from the same set of cards!)

- **At this point, use the cards as building blocks.** Build on each card, by expanding an idea into a sentence, a sentence into a paragraph. The stronger and more complete you can make each card, the easier your actual writing will be when the time comes. My experience has been that sometimes the report gets more than half finished while it's still on cards. Can't beat that.

As you study the cards, sometimes a phrase, a sentence, or even a whole paragraph may come to mind on how to develop a particular point. Stop and write the thought down directly on the card before those inspired words escape forever. That's why you might want to try using 5x8 cards, which offer much more space to write down your sudden thoughts. *(The Creative*

Organizer added 5x8 *scan pages* to their system several years ago, partly at my insistence.)

Often by the time you make these quick additions while arranging the cards in sequence, you'll have a big head start on the report.

That's it — the whole secret. It works so well it's almost scary. By comparison, if you had used a conventional approach, as soon as you had set down your ideas in even the most random of orders on a single sheet of paper, they would have begun to set harder than concrete and a whole lot faster. That seems to be the way human thought processes work: put something down on a page, and even though the order turns out (as random orders usually do) to be illogical or unworkable, your mind (subconscious?) works to justify (rationalize) its illogic. You often find the jumble impossible to change. You'll hate the helpless feeling of being stuck with an arrangement you know in your heart is wrong. Sad, but oh so true.

So, one more time: *Use the card system. Keep all your options open as long as you possibly can.*

Using Scan Pages

In the first edition of this book, I advocated using pocketed folders to organize. You doubtless know the kind I mean — bright-colored, with a pair of pockets inside to hold standard 8.5x11 paper, index cards, or what have you. In many ways, I still like these folders a lot, and I know a good many highly respected writers who use them. But I now have a system that suits me even better, and I think it's my duty to tell you about it. Here's the way I do it:

1. I use a separate (large) looseleaf notebook for each major writing project.

2. I organize all the cards I've assembled that relate to the project, and put them into *scan pages* that fit right in the notebook.

3. I use the *scan pages* as guides; this makes it very simple to come up with chapter headings, section headings, or whatever else seems appropriate for the job. Doing this is psychologically great for the user, because it helps you visualize even the largest job as a series of smaller tasks that you can easily complete a step at a time.

4. Put the appropriate cards into their respective *scan pages*. (You can get pages that are punched on both sides, so you can insert them as either righthand or lefthand pages. I like to start with the cards on the left side; as the material expands, I transcribe dictation, etc., put it on my word processor, and print out on regular paper. I punch the sheets with a three-hole punch and put them on the right side.

5. I use the material in each *scan page* to dictate more material for the typed pages. This is the way you start expanding that skeleton into a fleshed-out manuscript.

(**NOTE:** *Formerly, when I finished transcribing a tape, I would throw the tape itself into the folder. Now I have special binders that hold tapes and make them easy to catalog. At a later stage, you can refresh your mind if you have taken a topic through several editings or revisions, and want to check on your basic idea. This way you can trace everything back to rock bottom.*)

6. As the manuscript builds, work in "blocks." That is, try to write sections that are at least moderately capable of standing on their own feet without any extra explanation. Such blocks are handy because you can move them around quite freely without destroying your overall structure. Several times I have moved whole sections or even chapters around in this book; sometimes I've ended by moving them back again; sometimes not. But don't be surprised if your concept, or even your overall plan of attack, changes shape or focus as you really get into the work.

7. Set aside at least one *scan page* for miscellaneous or oddball material. If you dictate something that doesn't fit, or if you decide not to use it the way you had intended, **don't throw it away!** Put it in the oddball scan page. I learned this the hard way. Too many times I have gone prowling through the wastebasket to salvage something, only to find that it was gone forever — thrown out with the trash. I don't do that any more. If you are wise, you won't either.

Keep the *scan pages* — even when you have completed an entire first draft. (If you like, you can insert a rod that turns them into hanging files that fit any standard file cabinet.) You may end up by putting that first draft in its own notebook, and putting the next revision in a new one. This proved handy for me because I wanted to give you a couple of illustrations about how my own manuscript changed and was revised and rewritten through the various stages of editing.

Filling in the Gaps

As the book begins to take shape, the progress is evident. As long as a writer can see that the project is moving along, it is easy to keep up a full head of steam.

Well, that's most of it, but here's one more suggestion of a device that works for me. Maybe you'd like to try it.

When you're in a social situation, try bringing up your subject in casual conversation. For example, the week before Christmas 1979, Poggy and I went to a party and encountered a number of old friends from the K-G Players (a little theater group that we had belonged to for many years). When I told them I was writing a book on the art of dictation, they started giving me so many new ideas and suggestions that I had enough material for another couple of chapters.

One controversial matter that was aired heavily that night was time saving versus quality of work. Several of our friends said they preached the gospel of dictation as a device for time saving and increasing productivity, and were strictly in favor of getting things onto tape, off the tape onto he page, and out, without any messing around. Editing was overkill, they said.

Some of them said they dictated everything in "final form" and refused even to read the material over before signing it.

That almost sent me up in smoke. A few gifted dictators can doubtless use that technique and can get away with it. But in my opinion most of them can't, and shouldn't try to.

So I decided to increase the emphasis on the editing chapter. Granted, many of the professional dictating techniques I was describing are aimed first at saving time and increasing output. I absolutely refuse to concede that quality must suffer in the process. Part of the skill of the expert dictator lies — or should lie — in editing and tightening the dictated draft before it is printed out in final form.

Maybe it's because I've encountered so much poor dictation over the years. I wish you could see my "Rogue's Gallery" of examples on how *not* to do it; memos and letters that are poorly conceived, illogically constructed, miserably written, and impossible to understand.

Enough. As you can see, this sample of a discussion at a party makes a pretty good illustration of how things I learned in conversation eventually found themselves worked into the book. This was the fun part. In addition, as I've ready explained, I interviewed experts, read everything that I could find even remotely related to the subject (see Bibliography), and started mixing it all together.

By now, you know more about how this book was put together than I did myself — at least until I dictated the material for this chapter. An appropriate close is a quotation from one of my favorite lyricists, Lorenz Hart:

"If they ask me, I could write a book!"

*There's no limit to how complicated
things can get, on account of one thing
always leading to another.*
— E. B. White

16: Tips on Legal Dictation

Practice — The Best of All Instructors?

An old proverb tells us practice is the best of all instructors. Like many such proverbs, this one contains a basic truth. But educational psychology adds one important proviso: the practice must be performed correctly. All the *incorrect* practice in the world will do no good.

Ay, there's the rub. It explains why good dictators are so hard to find. Almost every dictator, good or bad, that I have interviewed has been self-taught; even the most skilled have achieved that skill primarily through trial and error.

Many of the problems of dictation are common to every line of endeavor. Difficulties are greatest, however, in disciplines involving professional expertise, a specialized vocabulary, or both. It is harder for scientists, engineers, physicians, and lawyers to dictate well than it is for persons in less technically exacting work.

Fortunately, however, many persons who practice these professions have superior gifts for expressing their thoughts fluently. Whatever other

problems they may have, dictaphobia is seldom one of them. Most of the professionals I've interviewed can dictate easily and glibly — indeed, perhaps *too* glibly. As they toss out their long, complicated sentences, studded with difficult technical words, they often make life miserable for their transcribers (I know whereof I speak; as part of my research, I have personally transcribed many hours of legal, medical, and scientific dictation.)

The Proof of the Pudding

There is nothing like transcribing actual dictation to ferret out problem areas. To discover legal and medical dictation problems, however, I had to solve another one first: where could I get some real-life examples? And what kind of examples would best serve my purpose? Private law firms or doctors in individual or even group practice may specialize in a particular kind of practice; the dictation produced in such environments might be only remotely applicable to most of my professional readers. Where could I find a useful cross-section? Once again, I sought the advice of the persons who know about such things.

And again I was lucky. My old friend Robert Allen suggested that the legal and medical dictation produced at the Veterans Administration (where Bob worked) might be an ideal subject for my study. Bob told me that VA relies heavily on dictation as the most practical available method of keeping up with the agency's enormous workload. Professional staff members — including large numbers of lawyers and physicians — spend a major portion of every working day at their dictation machines. The work is demanding and unusual, because it involves intimate familiarity with the terminology of both medicine and law. Under constant deadline pressure, VA physicians and lawyers must dictate rapidly, yet turn out documents that are medically accurate and legally sound — not exactly an easy task.

But the task of the transcribers is not an easy one either. Often the dictation is recorded in one city and transcribed in another. For example, the lawyers on the Board of Veterans Appeals record their cassettes at VA headquarters in Washington, D.C., but most of the dictation is transcribed in Wilkes-Barre, Pennsylvania. Because of this set-up, there is almost no opportunity for dictators and transcribers to communicate face to face. Under the constraints of this administrative arrangement, it seems remarkable that the documents produced by this "teamwork at long distance" usually turn out to be of such good quality – legally, medically, and technically.

Obviously, some problems are inevitable. To ensure accuracy, typed transcriptions (accompanied by the original cassettes) are returned to the originators for final checking. This process is time-consuming but absolutely necessary. Even when the original dictation is of the highest quality, mistakes sometimes creep in. When the dictation is "somewhat less than perfect" (to put it mildly) the need for careful checking increases – or disaster may result.

VA officials have long been aware of the problem, and have been seeking ways to correct it. Thus, when I explained my purpose to them, they cooperated freely in furnishing materials for my research. Bob Allen arranged for me to tell my story to Mr. Jack Blasingame, of the Board of Veterans Appeals. He and his staff, in turn, arranged for me to monitor and analyze a number of actual tape cassettes, and transcriptions from those cassettes. Without their cooperation, this chapter could never have been written – my thanks to all of them. We mutually hope that my findings and recommendations will be useful in improving the quality of VA's legal and medical dictation – and, indeed, of *all* professional and technical dictation, everywhere.

A Discourse On Method

As things turned out, I had let myself in for a tough week. My first task was to monitor and analyze my sample tapes, point by point, according to the Twelve Commandments of Good Dictation set forth in Chapter Six. First I checked for overall impressions: was the information well-planned and well-organized? Was the dictator's enunciation clear and easy to understand? Was the pace good? All I did at this point was listen – I made no attempt to take down a word-by-word transcription. That frightening step came all too soon.

Monitoring the tapes, I began figuring out a plan of attack and watched it begin to take shape. During the process, however, it changed several times right before my ears. Initially, I considered transcribing a few minutes from each tape, with comments on the good and bad points. When I tried a sample, I found the methodology could be instructive, but it also threatened to be unwieldy. Eventually I rejected the method as impractical.

I next considered analyzing each tape to see how it measured up to each of the individual commandments. This seemed promising until I tried it; then the idea fell apart. Still, I learned from both experiments, and they eventually led me to the method I now set forth.

I'm pleased to report that all the VA tapes I monitored showed evidence of good organization (COMMANDMENT I). From instructions recorded for the transcriber, I gained ample evidence that the dictators had thought before they spoke. This was further evidenced by the logical arrangement of thoughts and the generally well-constructed sentences. Thorough pre-planning was also frequently indicated by the fast pace of the dictation – in some cases much too fast! Several cassettes were almost impossible to transcribe. It was almost as if some of the dictators were issuing a challenge: "Come on, I dare you to keep up!"

My analysis of the VA tapes also showed that most of the dictators had done a reasonably good job on COMMANDMENT II; that is, they had put themselves into the "dictating frame of mind." Thoughts flowed smoothly and with little hesitation – BUT some of the voices sounded dull, flat, monotonous, and totally uninspired – deadly to listen to at any length.

Each tape I monitored was devoted to a single case. There was accordingly no need for COMMANDMENT III (indicate order of priority).

The example that follows is a "composite" dictation. It is *not* an actual transcription of any tape monitored – instead, it draws on elements from every one of them.

The entire sample dictation is set forth in a "typewriter style" type face (Courier 10-pitch, slightly reduced) and a narrower column width (with a "ragged right" margin) to make it easy to distinguish. The *instructions* to the operator are underlined, since most office style typewriters can't do italics. My comments on the dictation are set in the same type face and column width that you are reading now.

Sample Dictation

Hello, operator, this is Lee T. (as in Tango) Thistle, I spell T-H-I as in India S-T-L-E as in Echo, Room 000, Division XX, Extension 1234. On this cassette, my formal dictation is for copy beginning at the top of page two, standard Findings and Decision format, in the case of William J. Smythe. First name, William, middle initial J. as in Juliet, last name Smythe, S-M as in Mike-Y as in Yankee-T-H-E as in Echo, claim number 0123456. Operator, at the top of page two, please begin with a heading, all caps, centered, ACTIONS LEADING TO PRESENT APPELLANT STATUS. Dictation begins. New paragraph.

COMMENTS: "Operator" is a standard term for addressing the transcriber, and using the term is an excellent way to indicate *instructions*. If the dictator is personally acquainted with the transcriber, it is more "human" to address the person by name. In the VA situation, the term "operator" is preferred.

The dictator has immediately given *name identification*, which is good standard practice. I might note that on two of the cassettes I monitored, part of the name was not on the tape, so a warning is in order here. Most cassettes begin with a leader, about 10 seconds long, that is made of clear plastic and will not accept magnetic recording. Therefore, the dictator should make sure that at least 10 to 15 seconds are allowed to elapse after the cassette is started before actually beginning to dictate. I might also mention that some cassettes are now available that do not have leaders, or that have magnetic leaders; you can easily tell by a visual check. With a leaderless tape, you can begin dictation immediately.

Observe that the dictator used the phonetic alphabet, T as in Tango, for the middle initial, but did not use that alphabet in spelling out the individual letters of the last name, except for the few that might easily be misunderstood. There are several schools of thought on this; some say that the phonetic alphabet should be used throughout, each time spelling is required. Many of the operators I have interviewed disagree. They tell me that often the overuse of the phonetic alphabet leads only to confusion; many of the dictators do not know it well, and stumble over it.

There is still another problem, because there are several different phonetic alphabets that are widely used. The one I use naturally is now technically out-of-date, but millions of my compatriots who learned it in World War II know no other. The "new" version now used by the military has been the standard for years, but I find that many persons are nevertheless unfamiliar with it. In *Appendix A* I'll give you both versions for reference. Whatever phonetic alphabet you choose, I recommend that you use it only in cases where the operator is likely to confuse or misunderstand letters. The letters most likely to cause confusion are: A and **I**, **B** and **P**, and **M** and **N**. For these letters, I suggest you use A as in Alpha, I as in India, B as in Bravo, P as in Papa, M as in Mike, and N as in November.

(Dictation continues.)

> By rating action in January 1979, the
> veteran's service-connected os-
> teochondromatosis, I spell O-S-T as in Tango-
> E-O-C-H-O-N as in November D-R-O-M as in Mike-
> A as in Alpha-T-O-S-I as in India-S, comma,
> and post-(hyphen) traumatic, <u>I spell T-R-A as</u>
> <u>in Alpha-U-M as in</u> <u>Mike-A as in Alpha-T-I as</u>
> <u>in India-C</u> of the left knee was increased
> from a noncompensable rating to a ten percent

```
rating effective from October 6, 1968.
Period. new paragraph.
```

The veteran has filed a timely appeal from such determination. Period. <u>Operator, I want a new heading here, all caps, centered: CON-TENTIONS</u>. New paragraph.

It is contended by and on behalf of the veteran, in substance, that he is entitled to an earlier effective date for the assignment of compensable rating for his service-connected left knee disorder, to August 1976, at which time he quote first attempted to have my case reviewed period. End quote. New paragraph.

COMMENTS: As I have remarked earlier, most of the dictators did a good job of giving instructions (COMMANDMENT V). Each special instruction was introduced by saying "Operator," followed by the instructions, and ending with the statement "Dictation continues."

As for COMMANDMENT VI: SPEAK CLEARLY, I cannot give quite such a glowing report. I discovered wide discrepancies in this area. Some of the dictation was carefully enunciated and crystal clear. But in other cases, the voice faded in and out, as if the dictator were looking around in various directions or perhaps staring at the ceiling while continuing to speak. This bad habit can drive the operator crazy.

Several dictators also offended by loud sounds of breathing directly into the microphone. This fault is easy to remedy, but all too often dictators habitually do it, thus keeping their transcribers in a state of constant irritation.

As also mentioned earlier, some of the dictation was at an inexcusably fast pace, defying COMMANDMENT VII: PACE YOURSELF. This pouring out of great torrents of words may save time for the dictator, but it greatly increases the time it takes for the operator to decipher the words on the tape. And that, of course, is what the operator is there for. This heedless practice virtually guarantees that some of the words will be misunderstood and thus transcribed incorrectly.

I found that four of the six dictators monitored did well on COMMANDMENT VIII: PAUSE. They phrased in a natural way, with appropriate and meaningful pauses. The other two almost never paused but went hell for leather all the way. I attempted to transcribe at least five minutes of dictation from each tape I monitored. The difference in difficulty was instantly obvious. It's too bad some of the dictators don't occasionally play back a sampling of their own tapes; I can't believe they realize what a hard task they make for the operators.

I have already commented on COMMANDMENT IX: SPELL THINGS OUT, but one or two more remarks are appropriate here. The spelling — and the use of phonetics — were done in many different and irregular ways. Some dictators gave *only* the letters, while others used the phonetic alphabet on *every* spelling, to the point of confusion. My experience shows that letters pronounced carefully and clearly are almost as easy to understand as the phonetics, except for the borderline cases already discussed.

A couple of dictators used a curious mixture — sometimes letters, sometimes phonetics — with no apparent reason for the discrepancies.

Worthy of special mention is the fact that certain items — such as proper names — were usually spelled out. This is good. Unfortunately, however, some extremely difficult medical and legal terms were NOT spelled out. I did not have the faintest idea how some of these words should be spelled; I suspect that most of the operators would be in the same boat. I strongly recommend that dictators carefully spell out ALL difficult words — legal, medical, or technical.

All six dictators followed COMMANDMENT X: PUNCTUATE, fairly well. One small complaint: two of the dictators did not end their sentences with the standard inflections that one expects in normal speech. Instead, they ended with a rising cadence, more like that of a question; then the dictator would say "period" and catch the operator by surprise. I found this confusing, but eventually was able to get used to it. Nevertheless, I recommend that dictators strive to use the same inflections used in normal speech, even when giving the appropriate punctuation marks.

```
        (Dictation continues) . . . Operator, that
    concludes my dictation in the appeal of Wil-
    liam J. Smythe. This is Lee T. Thistle, Room
    000, Division XX, Extension 1234. Thank you,
    operator. Have a good day!
```

Some people tell me they think this expression is overdone and that nobody really means it. That may be; nevertheless, several operators have told me that they feel it adds a warm, human touch to what frequently may seem to be a somewhat inhuman operation. Accordingly, I recommend the practice, trite though it may be. A kindly, friendly ending may not make up for three or four hours of miserable and difficult transcribing, but it certainly does help.

From the VA tapes alone, I obviously can't tell whether the dictators follow COMMANDMENT XII: EDIT. I am told, however, that the practice is followed scrupulously. An accurate transcription is a must, and the only way the original dictator can be sure the tape was followed accurately is to check the transcribed copy when it is returned. Whether or not this step is used for anything other than checking accuracy, I cannot say. I hope that the dictators use the opportunity to clear up poorly constructed sentences and clarify meanings.

Summing Up

All in all, this experiment with actual VA dictation was an interesting, and for me, an enlightening, experience. I hope that my analysis and comments will help make the quality of this and other legal, medical, and technical dictation even better in the future.

Key points to remember, other than to follow the Twelve Commandments, are listed below:

- **Be especially careful in pronouncing and spelling out** difficult technical terms.

- **Watch out for pairs of words that cause confusion:**
  abjure, adjure; adverse, averse; apperception, perception; arraign, arrange; avoid, void; casual, causal; cite, site; collision, collusion; comity, committee; descent, dissent; defer, differ; disburse, disperse; dower, dowry; judicial, judicious; mandatary, mandatory; payor, payee; persecute, prosecute; precedence, precedents; prescribe, proscribe; presence, presents; thereon, therein; transferor, transferee; vendor, vendee.

  There are, of course, many others—these are just typical examples.

- **Use the phonetic alphabet when necessary;** see the listing in *Appendix A.*

- **Avoid reading totally written-out material directly onto the tape;** if you have the information already in written form, furnish it that way to the transcriber—it makes the job easier. Also, reading such copy tends to cause you to go too fast.

- **Monitor your own tapes now and then.** If you were transcribing, would you like the way you dictate?

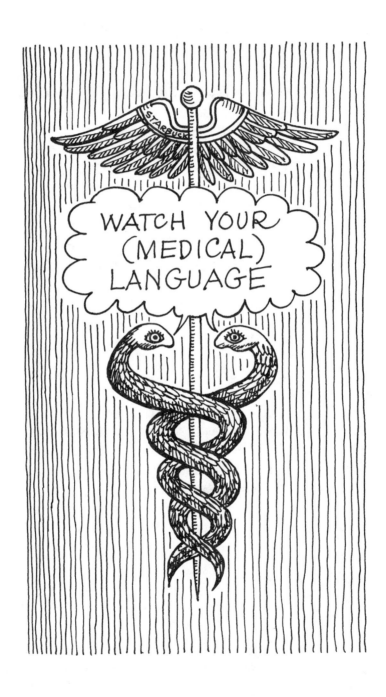

It should be the function of medicine
to have people die young as late as possible.
— Ernest L. Wynder, M.D.

17: Tips on Medical Dictation

Dictation — Just What the Doctor Ordered

Until I researched this book, I had no idea of the extent to which physicians use dictation to save time. They seem to recognize, perhaps more than many of the rest of us, how valuable time is, and they want to make the most of it. My friend Bob Allen told me that the Veterans Administration has long been a leader in using an organized system for medical dictation. As might be supposed, the VA has found that the problems of medical dictation are much like those of legal dictation — only more so.

Because medical dictation must of necessity be loaded with technical terminology, it is important for physicians and dentists to realize that transcribers are not always going to be able to get every word right. Some operators who have been on the job for years get extremely good at handling medical terms; with increasing experience, they need less and less help. These operators, however, are definitely in the minority. Many new transcribers enter the field each year, and these newcomers need all the

help they can get. Until they have learned the ropes, they need to have
difficult words spelled out for them, slowly, distinctly, and carefully.

Physicians must be especially concerned with clarity and good diction —
not to mention the spelling out of difficult words — when they are dictating
during hospital rounds. At such times there are likely to be background
noises or other distractions, and my samplings of tapes made under such
conditions indicate that many times words are garbled and the speed is
much too fast. Be aware of the natural tendency to "get on with the job,"
and take special pains to slow down and speak clearly.

Terms to Watch Out For

There is no way that I can give a complete list here of medical terms
most likely to cause problems for transcribers. The words below, however,
are typical examples, and all of them have been culled from tapes where
the operator heard them incorrectly. I would suggest that you familiarize
yourself with this list, and then add any words of your own that you use
frequently; check out some of the transcriptions of your dictation, and you'll
soon locate the trouble spots.

Okay, here's my list

ALLERGY (ALLERGIES)
ANEMIA
APPREHENSIVE
AREOLAR
ASPECT
ATYPICAL
BILATERAL
BASILAR RALES
BRONCHOSCOPIC
BROWN BUERGER CYSTOSCOPE
BRUIT
CARIES

CHADDOCK REFLEXES

CHIP FRACTURE

CONGENITAL

CONVERGENT

DORSAL SURFACE

EDEMATOUS

ETIOLOGICAL

EXPIRATORY

FIBROUS DYSPLASIA

FISHBERG CONCENTRATION TEST

FLORID FACIES

FRANK BLOOD

FUNDI

GLOTTIC CHINK

GREAT VESSELS

HOMAN'S SIGN

HERNIOTOMY

KAHN TEST

INTEREST

LIVER EDIGE

LYMPHATIC

MALAISE

MALODOROUS

NUCHAL RIGIDITY

OBLITERANS

OBTUNDED

OCCULT BLOOD

OPACIFIED

PALPABLE MASS

PEDAL EDEMA

PHARYNX

PLANTAR ASPECT

PROCTOSCOPIC

QUECKENSTEDT TEST

RIB SPREADER

RADIOLUCENT

RAPID HEARTBEAT

SCIATIC

SEROUS FLUID

SICKLE CELL ANEMIA

STRABISMUS

SUPINE

SUPPLE

TURBIDITY

TYMPANIC

ULCER CRATER

UNINVOLVED EXTREMITIES

WELL-NOURISHED

As I mentioned earlier, this list is incomplete, but representative. To get a better understanding of what happens to such words, I suggest you read through Appendix B after you finish reading this chapter. (Please finish the chapter first. Some of the material in Appendix B is so screamingly funny you may forget what the purpose of this chapter is intended to be.

Still, it isn't fair for me to keep you totally in suspense, so I'll give you a few excerpts here, with thanks and deep appreciation to Ms. Patricia Teernstra, who kindly gave me permission to quote here material in this book. Ms. Teernstra, who has a great sense of humor, has worked in a VA Medical Center for several years (I don't know exactly how many) and has put together a collection of mistakes in transcription. The sampling below will give you a good example of what can happen if you don't speak plainly and spell out difficult terms. But a sampling really isn't enough – hence, Appendix B. And I must say that Norman Cousins surely must be right when he says laughter is the best medicine. Ms. Teernstra's collection should cure almost any ailment known to medical science!

Some Examples of Garbled Medical Transcription

The first sentence is what the physician dictated – the second, what it "sounded like."

Sickle cell anemia
Sick as hell anemia

Patient had tarry stools
Patient had torrid stools

On assuming the upright position
Unassuming bright physician

Patient had a positive Homan's sign
Patient had a positive home inside

The x-ray was practically normal
The x-ray was frantically normal

How Can These Errors Be Avoided?

One might say that the answer to these problems is obvious. Still, sometimes the obvious is hard for us to see if we are dealing with a subject with which we are on extremely familiar terms.

So here I go stating the obvious again: please bear with me.

First of all, please follow the TWELVE COMMANDMENTS FOR GOOD DICTATION. Pay special attention to COMMANDMENTS VI through IX. To remind you: *speak clearly; enunciate; pace yourself* and don't speak too fast; *pause* when it is appropriate to do so; and *spell things out* any time you have an unusual word or name. Use the phonetic alphabet (carefully and sparingly).

In addition, you might want to do what many physicians have recommended to me – furnish your transcriber with a good medical dictionary.

(Some transcribers say this is overkill; they'd rather you simply furnish a list of the most-used terms.) With today's technology, you now have an even better choice: get your transcriber a software "spell check program" that has been especially compiled for the specialized medical vocabulary. Such programs can detect most mistakes in spelling, and frequently will also alert the user to wrongly used or confusing words. And they do all this automatically, with blinding speed. (**NOTE:** *If such a specialized program is not available for the particular word-processing program your transcriber uses, that's no big problem. Virtually every spell check program I know of can be customized; the transcriber can add words — making sure to see that they are correctly spelled — and the program will recognize the new words henceforth and forevermore. I "trained" my own software to recognize the specialized medical terms used here while I was putting the chapter through the spelling check that I always perform routinely before I press "SAVE."*)

And that's about it. Actually, in many ways you physicians have proved to be among the best dictators I have monitored. Your dictation is usually well organized and logical, and that's a good start. But few of us human beings are so good that we can't get better. I don't want to seem disrespectful of your high calling, but that goes for you, too, Doc!

If I sound either smart-alecky or preachy, I apologize. To make up for it, I suggest that, rather than removing the Appendix (B, that is), you read it. (Couldn't resist that.) It will brighten your day, and make up for all my homilies.

Hail and Farewell

And now my dictation draws to its close. I sincerely hope you've learned some new tricks and picked up some useful ideas and concepts. I had fun dictating it; I hope you had fun reading it.

Period. End of dictation. Have a good day!

APPENDICES

Appendix A

Phonetic Alphabets

Listed below are the two best known (military) phonetic alphabets. The version shown in the second column was used during World War II, and is now technically obsolete. It is, however, far more familiar (and hence more comfortable) to persons of my generation than is the current version. Because it's hard to teach old dogs new tricks, I thought it only fair to list both versions here. Also, in the real world I find that many dictators like to make up their own alphabets. Okay, it's a free country. I don't recommend the practice, but if that's your bag, I can't stop you!

> **NOTE:** *I strongly recommend that you use the phonetic alphabet only when there is danger of confusion or misunderstanding because of "sound-alikes." Many of the transcribers I have interviewed have told me that they believe overusing the phonetic alphabet is worse than not using it at all. The consensus: use the phonetic alphabet JUDICIOUSLY and SPARINGLY.*

NEW STYLE	OLD STYLE
ALPHA	ABLE
BRAVO	BAKER
CHARLIE	CHARLIE
DELTA	DOG
ECHO	EASY
FOXTROT	FOX
GOLF	GEORGE
HOTEL	HOW
INDIA	ITEM
JULIET	JIG
KILO	KING

NEW STYLE	OLD STYLE
LIMA	LOVE
MIKE	MIKE
NOVEMBER	NAN
OSCAR	OBOE
PAPA	PETER
QUEBEC	QUEEN
ROMEO	ROGER
SIERRA	SUGAR
TANGO	TARE
UNIFORM	UNCLE
VICTOR	VICTOR
WHISKEY	WHISKEY
X-RAY	X-RAY
YANKEE	YOKE
ZULU	ZEBRA

Appendix B

This material is drawn in its entirety from a collection of humorous mistakes in medical dictation collected over the years by Ms. Patricia Teernstra, Medical Administrative Specialist, Medical Administration Service, VA Medical Center, Wood, Wisconsin.

My thanks to Ms. Teernstra for permitting me to reprint major excerpts from her publication here. Thanks also to Robert Allen, who retired from the Office of Academic Affairs, VA Central Office, Washington, D.C. 20420. If he had not kindly brought this little masterpiece to my attention, I would never have known about it!

Below, in slightly abbreviated form, is Ms. Teernstra's collection, which is entitled

HAS THIS HAPPENED TO YOU?

To the new trainee in medical terminology, what the physician dictated and what she heard are two different "stories." Examples of what we mean are listed on the following pages. These have been saved through the years and nearly every new trainee here at Wood, Wisconsin, is represented.

The first sentence is what the physician dictated — the second, what it "sounded like."

There is pain on the plantar aspect.
There is pain on the platter aspect.

There is congenital shortening of the leg.
There is genital shortening of the leg.

The stool was guaiac positive.
The stool was wired positive.

The prostate was palpable on deep palpation.
The prostate was palpable on deglutition.

Patient was in the supine position.
Patient was in the sublime position.

Fever of unknown origin.
Femur of unknown origin.

Patient was discharged 6 days after herniorrhaphy.
Patient was discharged 6 days after delivery.

Bronchoscopic exam revealed a possible bronchogenic CA of right upper lobe.
Proctoscopic exam revealed a possible bronchogenic CA of right upper lobe.

X-rays were obtained.
X-rays of pain.

There were basilar rales noted.
There were dazzler rales noted.

There was bridging of bodies of L-l and L-2.
There was bridging of the valleys of L-l and L-2.

The abdomen revealed the liver, etc.
The abdomen was ill-delivered.

Patient was previously hospitalized at Brooklyn Naval Hospital.
Patient was previously hospitalized at Brooklyn Navel Hospital.

The patient slipped on a furry rug two weeks ago.
The patient slept on a fiery bath tub for two weeks.

RECOMMENDATIONS: Close observation until vital signs are stable.
RECOMMENDATIONS: Close observation until bottle sites are stable.

A duodenal ulcer could not be ruled out.
A duodenal ulcer could not be rolled out.

Temperature was borderline elevated.
The water line was elevated.

The patient had malodorous urine.
The patient had melodious urine.

The lungs were clear.
The lungs were square.

His throat was somewhat edematous and red.
His patient was somewhat edematous and red.

Bronchopneumonia, etiological.
Bronchopneumonia, theological.

Patient had pernicious anemia.
Patient had pernicious enema.

Hesselbach's triangle.
House of Ox triangle.

The paranasal sinuses were involved.
Pair of nasal sinuses were involved.

Histologically revealed. . . .
This logically revealed. . . .

The patient had mild diabetes.

The patient had vile diabetes.

Ethmoid sinuses.

Head point sinuses.

Fasting blood sugar was normal.

Fetus blood sugar was normal.

The pain was dull and boring.

The pain was darn boring.

The carotid arteries were palpable.

Corroded arteries were palpable.

Patient had syncopal episodes.

The patient had sinkable episodes.

The patient is strongly urged to contact AA.

The patient is struggling to contact AA.

Patient has frequent epistaxis.

Patient has creeping epistaxis.

The patient was a well nourished male.

The patient was a well married male.

Bowel sounds were normal.

Bubble sounds were normal. (Patient given soapsuds enema, so transcriber felt this was correct.)

The cough decreased in amount.
The cough decreased in the mouth.

Patient was given one unit of plasma.
Patient was given urine and plasma.

Patient had extrusive bowel movements.
Patient had exclusive bowel movements.

Feces were brown.
Fishes were brown.

The patient's hemoglobin was normal.
The patient's human globin was normal.

The patient has benign prostatic hypertrophy.
The patient has B9 prostatic hypertrophy.

Patient to use norisodrine inhaler.
Patient to use norisodrine in hair.

Patient was a cachectic white male.
Patient was a detective white male.

Patient had a port wine stain.
Patient had a port loin stain.

The over-all results were excellent.
The overhaul results were excellent.

There was an apical heart beat.
There was a pickle heart beat.

Patient had onychomycosis.
Patient had "honey comb."

The abdomen had shifting dullness.
The abdomen had shifting pelvis.

Mandibular and maxillary dentures were made.
Mandibular and auxiliary dentures were made.

On the 12th postoperative day the drains were turned and advanced.
On the 12th postoperative day the brains were turned and advanced.

Patient was prepped and draped in the usual manner.
Patient was prepped and raped in the usual manner.

There was no apparent enlargement to percussion.
There was no apparent logic to percussion.

The patient was followed by the Neurology Service.
The patient was fouled up by the Neurology Service.

Patient was given a pre-anesthetic evaluation by Anesthesia Department.
Patient was given a free anesthetic evaluation by Anesthesia Department.

The patient had loose stools.
The patient had blue stools.

The knee jerks were absent.
The kidney jerks were absent.

Patient had a perforated duodenal ulcer.
Patient had a perfect duodenal ulcer.

Mammary arteries.
Memory arteries.

Patient is to be given muscle re-education.
Patient is to muffle re-education.

Intact tympanic membranes.
Intact panic membranes.

The abdomen revealed a freely movable mass.
The abdomen revealed a frilly movable mass.

Resting 02 percentage.
Rust stain 02 percentage.

Patient is to have x-ray study of G.I. tract.
Patient to have x-ray study of G.I. crack.

The long leg cast was removed.
The long legged pants were removed.

There were moist rales in right lung field.
There were moist brows in right lung field.

Brown Buerger cystoscope.
Bomb digger cystoscope.

There was no AV nicking
There was no AV necking.

Zinc sulfate turbidity.
Zinc sulfates are bitter.

Patient should have x-ray study of the chest.
Patient should have serious study of the chest.

Fatty tissue and areolar.
Fatty tissue on a ruler.

There was a grapefruit size mass in the midline.
There was a grapefruit size mass in the mid-vine.

Pedal pulses were palpable.
Beetle pulses were palpable.

Patient had a temperature with malaise.
Patient had a temperature with blaze.

The liver edge was palpable.
The liver itch was palpable.

The patient had a rapid heart beat.
The patient had a rabbit heart beat.

There was a bruit in the chest.
There was a brewery in the chest.

RECOMMENDATION: Castellani's paint to nails daily.
RECOMMENDATION: Castellani's paint, two pails daily.

Patient was prepped and draped in the usual ,manner.
Patient was prepped and draped in a civil manner.

The greater saphenous system was mainly involved.
The greater saphenous system was mainly in the bowel.

The patient had convergent strabismus at age 7.
The patient had convergence to business at age 7.

The patient was sexually impotent.
The patient was sexually impudent.

General conditioning to uninvolved extremities.
General conditioning to unembalmed extremities.

The patient was discussed with the NP Department.
The patient was disgusted with the NP Department.

The knee is swollen, tender, red and warm.
The knee is swollen, tender, red and warped.

The bladder is never fully opacified.
The bladder is never fully pacified.

A rib spreader was inserted.
A red sweater was inserted.

There was a scar on the abdomen from previous grafts.
There was a scar on the abdomen from previous graphs.

The ankle was edematous
The ankle was edentulous.

Patient had the onset of back pain.
Patient heard the onset of back pain.

He was mentally obtunded.
He was mentally upturned.

The pupils and fundi were clear.
The pupils and front eye were clear.

He developed a toxic or alcoholic withdrawal delirium.
He developed a toxic or alcoholic growling delirium.

He developed a rash on the dorsal surface of the hands.
He developed a rash on the torso surface of the hands.

There was no nuchal rigidity.
There was no nuclear rigidity.

His affect was flattened.
His affect was flattered.

The lungs showed bi-basilar rales.
The lungs showed biceps rales.

Patient had a few expiratory wheezes.
Patient had a few excretory wheezes.

The patient had internal hemorrhoids.
The patient had infernal hemorrhoids.

There were marked atypical changes.
There were marked A to pickle changes.

There was marked obesity.
There was marked OBCT.

Bibliography

Adams, James L., *Conceptual Blockbusting.* New York: W.W. Norton & Company, 1979.

Barkas, J. L., *Creative Time Management.* Englewood Cliffs, NJ, Prentice-Hall, 1984.

Bates, Jefferson D, *Writing With Precision.* Washington: Acropolis Books Ltd., 1978, 1980, 1990.

Bruner, Jerome S., *On Knowing: Essays for the Left Hand.* Cambridge: Harvard University Press, 1956.

Buckley, Earle A., *How to Write Better Business Letters.* New York: Mc-Graw-Hill Book Company, Inc., 1957.

Calano, James, and Jeff Salzman, *Real World 101.* Boulder, Colorado, New View Press, 1982.

Collier, Robert, *The Robert Collier Letter Book.* Englewood Cliffs, N.J.: Prentice-Hall, Inc., 1950.

Cox, Homer, *How to Write a Business Letter (Rev. Ed.).* New York: Bell Publishing Co., 1956.

Frailey, L.E., *Handbook of Business Letters.* Englewood Cliffs, N.J.: Prentice-Hall, Inc., 1965.

Funk, Charles Earle, *Heavens to Betsy.* New York: Warner Paperback Library, 1955.

Ghiselen, Brewster (ed.), *The Creative Process.* New York: Mentor, 1963.

Gordon, William J.J., *Synectics.* New York: Harper & Row, 1961.

Jeffries, James R. and Jefferson D. Bates, *The Executive's Guide to Conferences, Meetings, and Audiovisual Presentations.* New York: McGraw-Hill, 1983.

Koestler, Arthur, *The Act of Creation.* New York: Dell, 1967.

Lakein, Alan, *How to Get Control of Your Time and Your Life. New York: Signet, 1973.*

Mackenzie, R. Alec, *The Time Trap: How to Get More Done in Less Time.* New York: McGraw-Hill Book Company, Inc., 1972.

Miller, Casey and Kate Smith, *The Handbook of Nonsexist Writing for Writers, Editors, and Speakers.* New York: Lippincott & Crowell, Publishers, 1980.

Mueller, Robert Kirk, *Buzzwords.* New York: Van Nostrand Reinhold Company, 1974.

Newman, Edwin, *A Civil Tongue.* New York: Warner Books, 1977.

Newman, Edwin, *Strictly Speaking.* New York: Warner Books, 1974.

Ornstein, Robert E., *The Psychology of Consciousness.* San Francisco: W.H. Freeman & Co., 1972.

Osborn, Alex, *Applied Imagination.* New York: Charles Scribner's Sons, 1953.

Rainer, Trisline, *The New Diary*. Los Angeles: J. P. Tarcher, 1978. (Distributed by Houghton-Mifflin.)

Rosenthal, Irving and Harry W. Rudman, *Business Letter Writing Made Simple*. Garden City, NY: Doubleday & Company, Inc. 1968.

Sheppard, Mona, *Plain Letters*. Washington, D.C: U.S. Government Printing Office, 1955.

Taylor, Harold L., *Making Time Work for You: A Guidebook to Effective Time Management*. Toronto: General Publishing, 1981.

Uris, Auren, *Mastering the Art of Dictation.* Houston: Gulf Publishing Company, Book Division, 1980.

Index